···AND THE···
FLESH
···BECAME···
WORD

···AND THE··· FLESH ···BECAME··· WORD

*Reflections Theological
and Aesthetic*

James VanOosting

A Crossroad Book
The Crossroad Publishing Company
New York

The Crossroad Publishing Company
16 Penn Plaza, Suite 1550, New York, NY 10001

Printed in the United States of America

This text of this book is set in 12/17 Galliard.

Library of Congress Cataloging-in-Publication Data
VanOosting, James.
   And the flesh became word : reflections theological and aesthetic / James VanOosting.
      p.   cm.
   Includes bibliographical references.
   ISBN 0-8245-2302-4 (alk. paper)
   1. Communication – Religious aspects – Catholic Church.
   2. Language and languages – Religious aspects – Christianity.   I. Title.
   BX1795.C67V36 2005
   230′.2 – dc22

                                                          2005009100

1   2   3   4   5   6   7   8   9   10   10   09   08   07   06   05

To

ROBERT REED
My stepfather

For our thirty-year ongoing conversation about jazz,
sailing, God, family, marriage, cocktails, politics, church,
"The Pacific," sons, cigars, tennis, Camp Pemi, careers,
sex, Vietnam, my mother, the Bible, Richard Nixon,
sports, lines & knots, credit cards, automobiles,
arcane vocabulary, bosoms, proper attire, fidelity,
the prostate gland, memory, and did I mention jazz?

And
As always
To

DAWN WILLIAMS
My wife

Whose every gesture and word assures,
"Never forget that you are loved!"

Contents

Contents

Preface

The twenty-four essays included in this volume were written over a period of thirty years, the first ("The Medium Is the Message: A View of the Incarnation") published in 1974 in *The Christian Century* when I was twenty-three years old. Their thinking glides back and forth along a double-tipped arrow implied by my title: *And the Flesh Became Word*. For the writer with a Christian perspective, the Incarnation is reversible. The sacramental transformations between flesh and word, word and flesh, circumscribe an ample space for grace. Many of these essays appeared originally in religious publications — a couple of them decidedly Protestant (*The Christian Century, The Reformed Journal*), a few markedly Catholic (*Commonweal, America, National Catholic Reporter*), and at least one virulently neither (*The Humanist*).

I'm tempted to say that essay writing isn't my primary occupation, but experience would belie. Given half a chance, I'll write an essay *before* a book, *after* a book, *between* books, and (my favorite) *instead of* a book. Writing an academic volume (five of 'em so far, and *that's it!*) gives me migraines. Writing a novel (four of 'em to date, with more to come) causes unabated heartburn. Writing an essay, by contrast, is an unadulterated hoot.

The same few subjects have recurred in my writing for thirty years now; hence, it's beginning to dawn on me that these must be *my* subjects or, more likely, my obsessions: the Incarnation, language, narrative, death, and the Communion of Saints. They play out in my fiction, as well. And, frankly, they're never far beneath the surface of academic work. These are the themes that drop vertically through the present table of contents. The horizontal lines are drawn somewhat arbitrarily, though not entirely so: (1) Personal Narratives, (2) Biblical Narratives, (3) Language and Theology, (4) Language and Work, (5) Language and Writing.

What thinking goes into any essay, at least for me, comes as much from conversation as from imagination. Hence, I want to thank the gorgeous conversationalists of my life. Dawn, Peter, Theshia, and Thomas — my family — are the best, day in and day out, simply the best. Kathi Best, my older sister, loves *everything* I write, and she never lies. Beverly Whitaker Long, Mary Frances HopKins, and Paul H. Gray are the world's three champion Interpreters of the Word. Sister Elizabeth A. Johnson, exhaustive research has concluded, is Miriam of Nazareth's *other* Cousin Elizabeth. John Hollwitz possesses the most incisive and grumpiest mind in American Catholic higher education. Robert Giroux, best luncheon companion in the galaxy, was the publisher without whom twentieth-century literature could just as easily have gone to heck. Chuck Rawlings has become my older (wiser) brother. Father James Cafone gives me intimations of what the voice of the historical Jesus must have sounded like — sweet. Lynn C. Miller has been my co-survivor of the academy for more than thirty years, and she's a wonderfully wicked writer. John Jones is a genuine *mensch* with editorial acumen. Thanks, all, for syncopating with me the sustaining rhythms of human conversation. Who could ask for anything more?

And now, may the words of my mouth and the meditations of my heart be acceptable to God, and amusing to you.

···AND THE···
FLESH
···BECAME···
WORD

PERSONAL
NARRATIVES

1

Kidnapped

From Baptist Playwright to "Catlick"

I grew up a fundamentalist Baptist in 1950s Freeport, Illinois. Although I was allowed to play basketball with Mikey Pohill, I couldn't go inside his house. The Pohills were Roman Catholic. If I saw a priest or nun walking toward me downtown, I crossed to the other side of the street. Priests and nuns were known to kidnap Baptists and force them to become papists.

Every August, Guy Libby came through our town and gave a tent revival. The final Saturday night, hosted at the First Baptist Church, was called "Pack-the-Pew Night." Each family was assigned a pew to pack with sinners. I was seven years old when my family won "Pack-the-Pew Night," overflowing into the Vosses' pew behind us, all on account of my inviting Miss Damier, my principal, and Miss Elgin, my sister's fourth-grade teacher, and almost all of our neighbors in a zealous door-to-door campaign. I did not invite the Pohills.

Guy Libby played two trumpets at the same time. A clear part of my calling to become a tent evangelist would be to play two trombones at the same time. Competitiveness is one of the gifts of the Spirit apparently edited out of St. Paul's list, but I possessed it in abundance notwithstanding.

The prize for winning "Pack-the-Pew Night" was that Guy Libby and Strat Shoefelt, his song leader, would come to your family's home for Sunday dinner the next day. You can't imagine my thrill at meeting these sacred celebrities in person. In truth, I can't imagine the thrill my mother felt when hearing the prize announced in front of a packed sanctuary. Could any cook have been more pleased, except, perhaps, Martha of Bethany?

I'm afraid the dream of becoming a tent evangelist rivaling Guy Libby proved short-lived. By fourth grade, I'd heard the call to play second base for the Chicago Cubs. (I would skip all Sunday games, of course, as a testimony.) This ambition took deep root until I came face to face with the sobering statistic of going 0 for 4 (years) in Little League. Even for an aspiring Cub, this probably placed the bar too low.

From Christian baseball player, I advanced to Christian trombonist (only one trombone by then, with loads of vibrato, along the lines of Mr. Bill Pearce, whose sacred trombone renditions could be heard over the airwaves of WMBI from Moody Bible Institute), Christian composer, Christian attorney, Christian missionary (preferably someplace with plumbing), and, finally, Christian playwright. This last was a turning point. Notice in each instance how the statement of my ambition asserted a parallel reality. In the lexicon of my Baptist boyhood, "Christian" was a magical adjective capable of converting a professional noun into a vocational calling.

I was a theater major in college, unlikely as that might sound on a fundamentalist campus. I got a good education, performing in eighteen plays over three and a half years, including works by Shakespeare, Molière, Ibsen, Chekhov, and O'Neill. I planned on going to the University of Minnesota for graduate school on a McKnight Fellowship in conjunction with the Guthrie Theater.

That's when it hit me. I was rehearsing Creon in Anouilh's *Antigone*. Walking back to my dorm room around midnight after a grueling practice, I suddenly realized, "I'm not becoming an actor after all. What I'm actually becoming is a writer." Much as I enjoyed performing, I loved rehearsal even more. The best part of acting for me were those six weeks of ingesting another's words, letting the speech, thought, and behavior of a character shape my own language, thinking, and attitudes. (Later, I would come to think of St. Paul's admonition to discipleship — "Put on the mind of Christ" — as, essentially, a performance metaphor requiring an actor's rigor and discipline.)

One of the great things about growing up Baptist is the reverence one develops for individual words. From earliest childhood, I can recall forty-five-minute sermons, twice each Sunday, on the eternal consequences of understanding a single noun, verb, or preposition. Preachers held forth on the authoritative interpretation of a biblical phrase, and I believed that salvation depended on the orthodoxy of one's grammatical parsing. I've been reading as if my life depended on it ever since.

For a fundamentalist, the act of writing, if engaged in at all, was thought to be more of a righteous crusade than an artful expression. The "word" served as an instrument of evangelism, as in preaching the word or teaching the word, and not as material for poetic, dramatic, or narrative discourse. And even if one wrote for the purpose of evangelism — witness today's bestsellers by Tim LaHaye and Jerry B. Jenkins — the idea was to do it quickly. Fundamentalists had little motivation to perfect their prose or to revise a phrase; utterance was propelled by apocalyptic urgency, eschatological giddyup.

Pursuing the writer's vocation put me into a theological quandary. As an aspiring novelist — I switched from the dramatic mode to the narrative under the influence of English novelist Charles Williams — I would join the fellowship of those sentenced to myriad tribulations in transit between the capital letter and the period, who weren't finished with a thing until it was done right, even if that meant forgoing the Rapture. The fundamentalist paradigm didn't provide any vocabulary for understanding narrative art.

Partly to fill this gap, in 1979 I became a Catholic. My long journey toward Rome was at turns both arduous and joyful. I was converted by converts — John Henry Newman, Gerard Manley Hopkins, Thomas Merton, and Dorothy Day. All four were articulate about their threshold experiences and provided the keys to unlock doors of sacrament, aesthetics, theology, and politics respectively. I recall from my Baptist boyhood the words to a Gospel song that began, "I love to tell the story." Sacrament — from historical Incarnation to daily Eucharist — teaches me how stories get told. Just as wine becomes blood and bread becomes body, a writer's words on the page lie in wait of transubstantiation. A sacred covenant between author and reader allows the possibility for "material" to transform into "element," borrowing Suzanne K. Langer's theoretical terms. Mere words on the page of a novel, say, can become lived experience, with the healing potential of incarnate grace.

The aim of art is not, fundamentally, evangelistic. All art is, essentially, sacramental, and the sacrament of narrative art is reversible. For the writer, flesh becomes word; for the reader, word becomes flesh.

Now, some twenty-five years later, I'm a giddy communicant who remains something of a bifurcated Baptist. More accurately, I'm either a Eucharistic evangelical or a Catholic who believes in sword drills. (A "sword drill," if you don't already know, is a ferociously competitive game pitting Sunday school children against one another in a race to find obscure biblical passages. I was skilled at this as a child and, if competition were available still, could probably win a few sword drills today. Once, in seventh grade, my Sunday school teacher challenged all of us boys to recite the books of the Bible faster than he — both Old and New Testaments in accurate, rapid-fire succession. I took Mr. Ohms by a full second, crossing the finish line in twenty-six and a fraction. For this feat, I won a frozen pizza with sausage. Even now, I prefer to recite the books of the Bible lickety-split. Slow me down, and I lose confidence.)

In 2000, I was in Rome for the "Jubilee for Artists," when Pope John Paul II expanded on themes articulated in the "Message to Artists" of Vatican II and his own letter to artists (1999). When inviting us to Rome, Archbishop Francesco Marchisano, president of the Pontifical Commission for the Cultural Heritage of the Church, penned this amazing sentence — part penance and part promise: "Even if in the recent past the church has found a certain difficulty in approaching contemporary art, she invites artists to come closer to her in order to assume once more their connatural ministry of spokesmen of the divine."

> *For the writer, flesh becomes word; for the reader, word becomes flesh.*

As a convert, I have found the Roman Catholic Church deeply hospitable. However, many bred-and-buttered "Catlicks" (Flannery O'Connor's spelling) have not, apparently, and I suppose I can understand why. Artists — whether novelists, sculptors, or musicians — have always been cautious of orthodoxy, uncomfortable with creed. I don't know if the Roman Catholic Church is any more onerous in its orthodoxy or crushing in its creeds than a fundamentalist Baptist church. But there certainly are more Catholic artists than there are Baptist ones. This is true, partly, for historical reasons. The church used to pay good money for great art. More important, Catholics have a near corner on sacrament, the essence of art.

23

In the 1960s, Austin Farrer, warden of Keble College, Oxford said, "The process of artistic invention probably casts as much light as anything human on God's devising of the world." If this be so, providing artists of faith with a greater comfort zone in the Roman Catholic Church should prove mutually enriching to the body of the artist and the body of Christ alike.

I was talking with my mother on the phone one night, reminding her of the terrible silliness of my boyhood paranoia toward Catholics. (Mother is now an enlightened Presbyterian living in Florida; hence, we can joke about our spiritual blindness of bygone years.) "Remember, Mom, when you used to tell me that Catholics would kidnap a Baptist?"

"Yes," she said, "I remember."

I laughed. "Whatever possessed us to believe such a thing, do you think?"

Mother did not laugh. "We believed it, Jimmy, because it was true."

2

To Friends of the Library

I wonder if I'm alone in having taken a shine to librarians and libraries even before I warmed up to books? My earliest crush was on a white-haired beauty named Mrs. Popp, children's librarian at the Freeport Public, who read to us first- and second-graders in the basement while our mothers prowled the adult stacks upstairs. The sound of her Saturday-morning voice mingles in my recall with the athletic echo of basketball games played on the YMCA court (to which most of us boys went directly from the library) and with the sweet melodies of Sunbeam Choir rehearsal at the First Baptist Church (where only two of us had to go after the Y). Mrs. Popp, head-to-toe, was better by a long shot than the basketball coach and, God knows, much to be preferred over the choir director. Among these great buildings — the Y, the church, and the library, all of them red brick — the Freeport Public was my holy of holies.

To tell you the truth — which wasn't always my custom as a boy — I'd have to sort through a lot of library memories before ever hitting on a book. Take, for instance, the feel of possessing my own borrower's card — as orange as Ellen Eade's hair and every bit as legal as a driver's license. I remember receiving it over the high counter of the front desk in a quiet ritual that would make *The People's Court* look like some shady side show. Carrying that card in my hip wallet promised privileges of adult magnitude. At the same time, it held the constant threat of my financial ruin. At two cents per day, an overdue book could cut deeply into any week's allowance. The few times I remember having to pay a book fine were occasions of mortal shame, each one — Mother's shame first and then my own. She made me approach the bench all by myself and fess up. I really do believe that if all members of Congress had had library cards when they were children, and if each had had a mother like mine, not even the dictionary would carry "national deficit."

My grandparents were library patrons of the first order. They would go there as regularly as I went to church, and with a good deal more devotion. That building — along with its contents, its personnel, and its hallowed grounds — was sacred to them. When I was in the third grade, Grandma ran for public office to become a member of the library board. And she campaigned hard, believe me. On election night, the whole family, together with some close friends, gathered at her big house on Stephenson Street to listen to the returns by radio. On the half-hour, an announcer broke into the story of Kennedy versus Nixon and gave us updates of the races for school and library boards. I would like to say that we also had a chalk board in the living room for calculating phone-in returns district-by-district, but I could be wrong about that. The thing that I can't forget all these years later is that Grandma lost. Some hoodlum nosed her out in a photo finish. She took this defeat, like everything else, with measured grace. Not me. I was bitter. Still am. That election to the library board taught me a hard lesson about democracy: the best candidate doesn't always win.

I believe in the sainthood of all readers.

It's embarrassing to mention all the ways that I like books. I like to feel 'em — cover, binding, and paper. I like to smell 'em — glue, ink, and invisible semantic mold. I try not to taste 'em, but sometimes I can't help it. And, of course, I like to read 'em — combining the pleasures of eye and ear, leaning in close to listen and see.

If a person were interested in trains, I'd point the way to Chicago's Union Station. If they were into crawfish, I'd insist on their going to Pat's in Henderson, Louisiana. If they wanted old-world hospitality, I'd recommend the Hotel Algonquin in New York City. But for those of us into books, there's only one place to hang out.

A library, for me, is the Grand Central Terminal of human experience. It's a place for embarking in wonder and returning in wisdom. Get on board a library, and you can travel even farther than the green-and-gold dream machine of my boyhood — the Land O' Corn on the Illinois Central.

From my first acquaintance with the Freeport Public, through years of intimate affairs in school libraries, university special collections, the Edinburgh holdings in English-language fairy tales, and all the way to the Library of Congress itself, I'm hooked — word, line, and thinker. I still can't help making a boyhood link between the First Baptist Church and the library. My creed remains what it's always been — that the home of literature is a cathedral of grace and not a temple of doom. I believe in the sainthood of all readers, suffering first the little children to come onto books.

3

The Game and the Shame of Storytelling

Truth to tell, I couldn't play the game. Not well. This much of my story, I feel pretty certain, is correct. In the outfield, I lacked judgment. At home plate, I lacked courage. On the bench, my natural position, I lacked . . .

But here the tale begins to tilt. Can you feel it? And I don't want it to tilt. I can tell I'm beginning to get off base because of the parallelism. "In the outfield. At home plate. On the bench." You shift the preposition, substitute the noun. It's a sucker pitch. Don't swing at it. Just take it, trust me. Sometimes, I worry that as a storyteller I prefer symmetry to truth. Style confuses me, morally.

So, start again.

I couldn't play the game. Not well. But I could *narrate* it well. This I was very good at. Ask my dad.

Every day for two summers — between fifth and sixth grades, and again between sixth and seventh — I sat on our big front porch on Johnson Avenue listening to my six-volt transistor radio, that red and silver job about the size of an electric razor, tucked inside a case of genuine leather. Very snappy. Vince Lloyd and Jack Quinlen broadcast the Cubs' games from Wrigley Field. This was before lights, of course, which is the reason I was listening to those games every afternoon. When Dad got home from the bank, he'd always want to know, "How'd Holtzman do today? Did Williams extend his hitting streak?" And I liked to be prepared.

I kept a detailed, accurate score card. Designed the thing myself with neat boxes squared into straight columns on notebook paper. I dated each one in the upper-right-hand corner, and titled it by the Cubs' opponent for the day: Dodgers, Reds, Cardinals. Keeping score that way, for my father, introduced me to the pleasures of narration — selecting highlights, retelling key hits, critical errors, and putting my audience into play. That was the best part. Seeing Dad nod his head in participation, squint his eyes, picturing that 5-4-3 double play, from Santo to Hubbs to Banks. (Ah, Kenny Hubbs. What a tragedy, huh?)

The Cubs are, more or less, the sum total of what my father and I share in common. And they are sufficient. Between us, he and I know generations of Cub players like some people know their family trees. We used to analyze whether George Altman would ever develop a glove to go along with that big bat of his, or if Ernie's move from short to first would add three, maybe even five years, to his career. We revered Mr. Wrigley like a patriarch. Mind you, that was when the word still meant something good, such as Moses, or Elijah, or Lou Gehrig.

 I couldn't play the game. Not well. But I could narrate it well.

But I'm listing again. You can feel it, can't you? I was trying to tell you about the pleasures of narration. Getting the details just right, the sequence of things, that's pretty important. But it's not as important as *why* you're telling the story in the first place. The secret is hidden inside the folds of a soft woven fabric, under which, like a warm blanket, storyteller and listener snuggle together, skin against skin, body touching body. This deep-down pleasure of narration, so close to decadence you can't ever be sure, is called intimacy. That was my dad and me, so many years ago, between my fifth and sixth grades and again between sixth and seventh, when the story was about the Cubs, but the story*telling* was all about father and son, huddled together under the comforter

31

of a tale exchanged, sometimes twice told, time and again, worth repeating, but matchless still.

If it was telling stories *for* my father that taught me the pleasures of narration, it was telling stories *on* my father that taught me its shame. At the same time I was narrating the Cubs day in and day out, I was also keeping score on my father — day in, day out. And I wasn't telling those stories to just any audience, oh no. I was telling them to a consumer, to a customer, my mother. And I am sorry to say — sorrier than I *can* say — that I exercised all of my youthful creativity to make sure that customer was satisfied.

The arrangement with my mother went on the year round, but the greatest pressure came during the summer. In fact, during those same two summers when I narrated our beloved Cub games to Dad, I was betraying him when I made my daily surveillance reports to Mom.

Dad drove home from the bank every day about 4:30, down Springdale, which borders our town park where Little League games were played. The mission Mom recruited me for was to pedal my bike to the park late every afternoon, usually right after I snapped off the radio from the Cubs' game. At the park, I would hide behind the broad trunk of one of the big maple trees lining Springdale Avenue.

At the corner of Springdale and Hillcrest, right next to the Burlington commuter tracks, stood a modest, brick, two-flat rental. On the second floor lived a woman, let's call her Rachel. She was a secretary at my father's bank. He used to drive her home every day from the office. What Mother wanted to know was what time the car pulled up, and did Dad go inside with Rachel? If so, how long did he stay there, and could I see anything through the picture window? If not, how long did they sit there together in the car and talk? She wanted minutes. She needed exact times. She relished details.

My spying constituted an undercover operation, of course. If Dad had spotted me, I had a contingency plan to hop on my bike and ride off just as casual as could be, probably waving to him. But I knew if I ever had to call Plan B into action, the jig would be up. My cover would be blown. He'd go underground like a mole.

In a way, composing and telling those two different stories — recounting the Cubs' game for my father and reporting Dad's game for my mother — were similar. Both demanded close observation on my part. Both involved keeping score. My records, in each case, were impeccable. Down to the minute. Down to the second. I used the sweep hand.

To this day, I sometimes wonder what Dad must have thought when I pedaled my bike up our driveway, arriving five minutes *after* he got home, no matter what time that might have been. He never asked where I was. I have this haunting recollection of the look he'd give me when I strolled through the back door, sweating to beat the band but feigning nonchalance. He was not a dumb man.

He'd look at me in silence, reading into my eyes, but never asking what was there. After a moment, he'd gin up a genuine smile, sometimes clap me on the shoulder, and ask, "How'd Holtzman do today? Did Williams extend his hitting streak?"

I never felt so important, so appreciated, so at-one with my old man as during those fifteen minutes of storytelling.

That was my cue to grab my scorecard, and we'd go into the living room together, sit down on the sofa side-by-side, and I'd tell him the story: inning by inning, top half, bottom half, change of pitcher, pinch-hitters, what direction the wind was blowing, and how many times Randy Hundley took on the home plate umpire. Dad listened with a mixture of patience and enthusiasm, cherishing the details, exchanging the currency of a bank executive's day for the narrative melody of "Take

Me Out to the Ball Game." I never felt so important, so appreciated, so at-one with my old man as during those fifteen minutes of storytelling, relating a tale in which neither of us had anything at stake, but which both of us deemed the highlight of the day.

It wouldn't be till the next morning that I'd turn mercenary and sit down in the kitchen with my mother to tell her that other tale. "Well," I'd say, flipping through mental notes from yesterday's observations, "the car pulled up at 4:37. They both got out."

Mother would interrupt me. "Did he open her door for her?"

"Yep," I'd say, regretting having left out this detail myself. "Yep, he walked around the car and opened her door."

Mother would shake her head in angry confirmation. It was just as she suspected.

"And they walked up to her apartment *together*," I'd say, giving the word a sinister twist.

"Arm in arm?" Mom would ask.

"No," I'd say, "but together."

She nodded again. I was giving her what she wanted.

"And then they went inside," I'd continue. "The door closed, and they went upstairs."

Sometimes Mom would close her eyes, imagining the scene as I described it.

"I could see Dad through her picture window. Standing with his back toward me."

"Where was Rachel?" Mom would ask.

"Hard to say. I couldn't see her."

"Ah-hah," Mom would confirm, nodding her head, placing Rachel somewhere in the private showing of her own fantasy.

"Then Dad moved away from the window," I would report. "And I couldn't see what happened next." I'd adopt a tone of voice that suggested anything at all might have happened next, and probably did. It was better for my mother not to know.

"How long?" she'd ask.

"Seven minutes," I'd answer, as if the number held significance, as if it were telling.

Day after day, I kept my log. Day after day, I reported to Mom. All she needed from me, really, were a few narrative pegs on which she could hang the soiled laundry of her own longing, of her own boredom, of her own need. Even as a youngster, I knew what we were doing between us. I knew my own culpability, my own part in allowing her to take the ball and run, even if in the wrong direction.

And now, as a middle-aged novelist, my profession is to tell stories, to write stories, to take notes, to compose fictions. For others. And what could I say that I learned from a childhood of serving my listeners and, at the same time, betraying them?

Well, I learned that it takes two to make a story, and that there are usually third parties lurking unseen.

I learned that you can hurt yourself while giving someone else narrative pleasure and, truth to tell, you can pleasure yourself while giving someone else pain.

I learned that the demands of a listener can be just as vaunting as the ambitions of a teller.

I learned that in composing others, you end up composing yourself.

And I learned that the pains of storytelling are more instructive than its pleasures, that the wounds that storytelling can inflict are real, that the scars run deep, and that the only hope of healing is to story some more, to story again, to re-vise, to re-write, to re-mind one's own body that in the beginning was not the breath, not the heartbeat, not the brainwave, not the sex act; to re-mind one's own body that in the beginning, once upon a time, was the word. And every time we story together — whenever two or more of us story together — that word is made flesh, and it dwells among us.

4

About Nintendo

It's a double embarrassment to have to admit that I became hooked — push button, joy stick, and power pad — on home video games. First, as a parent, I had held the Christmas party line against Nintendo. We'd trained our sons — then thirteen and six — so well that they were grateful when my wife and I agreed to *rent* one. But that plan got scuttled because a couple of generous friends from Scotland offered to spring for the entire gift-wrapped package. I figured that the halo effect of their purchase might cast a glow on me, so, in saying thanks, I became an unwitting pusher of my own addiction.

My deeper embarrassment, though, was all wrapped up in what it meant to be a modern man. See, I was no nickel-and-dime junkie, smoking or snorting every high-tech weed in the joint. No, no. My habit was low-down patriarchy and high-class chauvinism. I could not stop myself, I swear, from rescuing princesses. Every day, come what may, I would get on my electronic charger and buzz off to release a damsel from her danged distress.

One of the curses of being brought up as a male WASP in the 1950s is to have been blessed with a mother of overweening gentility. She indoctrinated me to stand up when a lady enters the room, to open car doors, to give way at elevators, to slide a woman's chair in and out at the dinner table, and to shake hands only if she offers hers first. I didn't learn these lessons intellectually, as one might memorize the capitals of Europe. I grasped them muscularly. Mother's code of gender civility got printed into the synapses of my central nervous system. As a nine-year-old boy, I could be sitting with my back to the door and tell you if a lady or gentleman had just entered the room. I'd know this because I'd find myself standing up like some robot, levitated by the instinct of mother's good breeding. She was proud. My legs were strong.

Now, in a different era, those muscle memories are lethal. Any female takes her life in her hands when walking through a doorway with me. If I'm tired after a long day at the office, or just plain not thinking, I'm apt to lunge for the door and open it smack into an on-coming face. At such moments, I'm always thoroughly ashamed of myself and apologize profusely. And at the dinner table, I've learned to cover my shame by pulling out *everybody's* chair.

Before contracting my new video virus, I thought I was doing fairly well on retooling my masculine sensibilities. But then — thanks to Mario, Luigi, and the princess — I relapsed into the warp zone of prefeminist chivalry. My addiction, like any other, began innocently enough. I simply wanted to be with my children while they were learning their new game. I suppose I could trace the whole problem back to World One, Level Four of Super Mario Brothers.

 My habit was low-down patriarchy and high-class chauvinism.

In short order, I'd acquired all the knightly skills necessary to slay Bowser, that mythic beast guarding the Princess Toadstool. I could squish Little Goombas, jump on Koopa Troopas, clip the wings off Paratroopas, and hop over the Buzzy Beetles. So when I grabbed that magical axe to cut down the evil Bowser, I was chock-full of myself. Such a shock, you can imagine, when I read the disheartening message on the television screen: "Thank you! But our princess is in another Castle." Well, I was dumbfounded. Where the heck was that princess? I asked our seventh grader to call all of his friends, immediately.

Wouldn't you know, the Princess Toadstool was in World Eight, Level Four. So we set out on a two-week quest like some Arthurian tag team — kindergartener, middle schooler, and old man — to rescue that princess. As we conquered new worlds, the three of us boasted of our heroic exploits and took secret oaths of renewed fidelity. Each unexplored level required more wily strategy, better eye-hand coordination, and firmer resolve. We researched. We brainstormed. We read manuals and magazines. We consulted experts and buffs. We ran up our long-distance telephone bill.

I personally got past the Hammer Brothers and found extra lives. I learned the botanical mysteries of man-eating Piranha Plants and the aquatic moves of Cheep Cheeps. I learned how to super-speed, launch off the jumping board, and master-mind a bulldozer attack. You name it, and I could do it.

The day finally came when we got to World Eight, Level Four and confronted that ultimate Bowser head-on. My older son tried jumping over him, the younger one ran under him, and I shot him with fireballs. This combination worked like a charm. Prime Evil bit the dust and our Princess Toadstool just gushed with pleasure. "Thank you, thank you, thank you!"

Personally, I was overjoyed too — in a courtly, modest sort of way, of course. Just a couple of high fives, a split of champagne, and strawberry shortcake for dessert.

Then came the rub.

It wasn't till the next day that I realized what an addiction I'd fallen victim to. The boys forgot the princess. They assumed new roles and took on new challenges, becoming dream characters in *Super Mario Brothers 2,* swordsmen in *Double Dragon,* and Olympians in the *World Class Track Meet.* They tried to persuade me to come along *Duck Hunting* or to take *Simon's Quest.* And when I refused, saying that I'd prefer to rescue the princess again, they even volunteered to take a sacrificial whack at video baseball or golf. No way. That's when I knew I was hooked. This addiction, which they couldn't understand, was more deeply rooted in the psychology of my own boyhood than in the technology of theirs.

"Come on, Papa," they cajoled. "You've already rescued that princess. Why not go with us after Wart now?"

"Who is this Wart?"

"He's the monster in our new quest. You'll love him."

"Has he captured any princesses? Does he lock up damsels in his dungeon?"

"No, no, nothing like that. He has this really bad dream machine. It's really great. And he gives Mario and Luigi and Toad super nightmares."

"He doesn't take a single princess hostage?"

"Nope."

"Well, I don't think so, fellas, but thanks anyway. I'll just stick to what I know best."

[Pause.]

"Papa?"

"What?"

"It's getting kind of embarrassing, you know?"

"What is?"

"Your rescuing that princess all the time. You've saved her three times today already."

"So?"

"Don't you ever get tired of it?"

"Sure I do. But she needs me."

"It's just a game, Papa, a silly video. She doesn't care whether you rescue her or not."

[Another pause, this one pregnant.]

"Come again?"

"You're taking this thing far too seriously. Some of our friends are beginning to talk on the school bus."

"What did you say? She doesn't *care*?"

"That's right. She probably enjoys living with Bowser. Your princess is just an actress playing a part. Leave her alone."

"I'm sorry if I embarrass you."

"Don't worry. Anyhow, it's partly our fault. If we'd known you really believed in all this stuff . . ."

"Please, I don't need your pity. What is it your friends are saying about me, by the way?"

"Oh, it doesn't matter really. Just so long as you're getting better, that's what counts. Now, you're going to leave that princess alone, right?"

"Sure, sure. But tell me what they're saying. It might prove interesting."

"Our friends just think you're a little bit dated, okay?"

"Dated? They actually said 'dated'?"

"You know, old-fashioned."

"Me? Old-fashioned? Me, who can get to 8 – 4 at will, when most of your friends can't get out of World One? I'd like to know what they mean by 'old-fashioned.' "

"Like some character in one of those 1940s movies that Mama likes to watch."

"I see."

"No offense, okay?"

"It's quite all right, guys. I appreciate your telling me. I'll work on changing my rating."

"You don't have to change a thing, Papa. Just knock it off with the princess."

"All right. I get the message. I can quit anytime."

"And would you mind not talking about her when our friends come over?"

"No problem."

"Thanks, Papa."

"Don't mention it."

So, to the world at large, I stopped playing video games. I went back to teaching performance studies to graduate students, writing novels for young readers, and rooting for my Chicago Cubs — acceptable fantasies, all. Only late at night, after everyone had gone to bed, did I slip downstairs to slide that prohibited cartridge into the video slot and light up my fateful addiction once again. Usually a single fix would do me. But sometimes, when I was desperate, I would rescue her twice in a row.

Who is to blame for this affliction? My mother? Messrs. Nintendi? Our old-world friends from Edinburgh? Me?

I tried going cold turkey off my low-tech romanticism and simply couldn't do it. I needed help — an organization for Quixotes Anonymous. Or, maybe, somebody out there would come up with a feminist video game that reprograms insatiable princess-rescuers.

5

Death and Resurrection

I've only died twice. This happened nine years ago when I was forty-five — and both times it was painless. I was in San Diego, California, visiting a co-author on the morning of September 11, 1996, when I awoke with the beginnings of a migraine. Mentioning this to my hostess at breakfast, she recommended I try an extra-strength Motrin before resorting to my usual prescription antidote. I swallowed one. My colleague and I drove off to Kinko's to copy some manuscript pages and en route back to her house I commented, "My hands feel itchy." Glancing over at me in the passenger seat she said, "Your hands must be way more than itchy. Just look at them." They'd swollen to the size of catcher's mitts. I never knew skin had so much give.

No more than twenty seconds passed between the onset of feeling itchy and my declaring, "I can't breathe." That was the last thing I remember. The sensation of not being able to breathe was uncomfortable, but I wouldn't describe it as painful. The moment passed quickly, as did my consciousness.

I learned the details of what later occurred from my colleague and the physicians and workers in the hospital emergency room. I became a mere character while they narrate for the next part of this story.

My colleague executed a 180-degree turn and drove in excess of a hundred miles per hour on the shoulder of the freeway — against traffic — and then pulled a U-turn up an off-ramp to the nearest hospital. There, a trauma team of seven doctors, nurses, and technicians, currently idle, rushed to the car at the entrance of the ER. They opened the passenger door, unclasped the seat belt holding me upright, and lifted me onto a gurney.

My heart had stopped beating and the technicians referred to me as having died. They then did that electrical thing to the heart that you see on TV — defibrillating, I think it's called — as well as some other medical stuff, and eventually, about two hours later, I regained consciousness. I was put in a private area in the ER and hooked up to lots of machinery. They had "cut off" my clothes and, apparently, I'd soiled myself — which is one of the truly embarrassing things about dying.

Over the next few hours I became conscious in a twilight state and grasped the gist of what had happened to me (it's called anaphylactic shock), what was happening to me now (the unidentified, toxic allergen was continuing to attack), and what was likely to happen to me soon (I was expected to die again, this time for keeps). All the doctors were excited, and I received their rapt attention. From a physician's point of view, anaphylaxis is an intriguing phenomenon. It's about the only situation in which a perfectly healthy person's organs all shut down simultaneously. Furthermore, it's unusual for a victim to survive one of these deals.

Apparently, I'd soiled myself — which is one of the truly embarrassing things about dying.

I'm told I was unable to speak while in the ER, although I distinctly recall trying to apologize for making a mess. I don't remember being transferred to the intensive care unit, which happened sometime in the late afternoon. But I do recall coming fully awake while there.

My entire body was swollen with medical paraphernalia attached to my arms, chest, and face that restricted my movement. Otherwise I was in no pain. I'd always wondered what it felt like to be a patient in ICU. I looked around at the bodies lying on other beds and hy-pothesized what ailed each of them. I met allergists and infectious disease specialists and answered all their questions. They were fighting the clock to find out what was attacking my body and, I gathered, they were losing. Their greatest suspicion focused on a herbicide applied to a lawn I had walked across that morning.

I found lying in the ICU to be restful and contemplative. I determined I was happy, more or less, with the forty-five years I'd been given. I would have liked to have seen my boys — then twenty and thirteen — grow to adulthood, but I could already detect the pattern of their development, and I was pleased. I thought I had some more writing in me — better stuff than I'd yet written — but I was grateful for the length of time I'd been allowed to work as a professional writer. All in all, if the angel of death wanted to swoop into San Diego's Alvarado Hospital and fly me away, that was okay. (I know this sounds flippant but, honestly, it's the way I felt. No complaints. Ready to go. Content in the moment.)

About 2:00 a.m. on September 12, 1996, my heart stopped beating again. First I heard the steady beep, beep, beep of the heart monitor go silent. Then I glanced over at its visual readout and saw the spiky line go flat. This couldn't be good news. I heard voices shouting, "Code Blue, Code Blue!" I saw doctors and nurses running toward my bed. All of this took only a second — maybe a fraction of a second — between the moment my heart stopped pumping and the time oxygen was cut off to my brain. I remember thinking, "Damn it. I'm going to die as a TV cliché. I've seen this scene a hundred times." Then, just before losing consciousness, I was amused by the view I had of the situation and said to myself, "But this 'camera angle' is cool. I don't remember ever seeing a code blue with the lens shooting directly from the patient's eyes."

Then blankness.

I'm not sure what they did to resuscitate me. Whatever it was, I was gone for four hours. Nope, I didn't see any tunnels, bright lights, or welcoming angels. Nor, thank goodness, did I hear the lapping water of the River Styx.

I emerged from a light coma around 6:00 a.m. On the right side of my bed stood an allergy researcher. To my left stood a cardiologist. At the foot were two former graduate students of mine. (Don't ask me how they got there.) They were all engaged in a lively conversation, and the cardiologist was talking across my body with animated gestures to the allergist. "Listen," he said, "I come from South Africa. I know *villages*. And believe me, it doesn't take a village." (Hillary Clinton's book *It Takes a Village* was on the best-seller list at the time.)

I got excited thinking, "Fantastic! Heaven includes rhetorical criticism." I honestly believed I'd entered a happy afterlife. When I inserted myself into the doctors' conversation with a comment about metaphor, all four bystanders jumped.

It took a few minutes for me to piece together that I wasn't dead after all — that I was still in ICU and that my heart must have started ticking again. I stayed there for a week while blood samples and test results were sent through cyberspace hither and yon, from laboratory to laboratory. I ceased being so intrigued with the conditions of fellow patients and the procedures of an ICU. The only distinct memory I have is of a brief telephone conversation with my mother. I called her in Florida to tell her what had happened. I explained that I was in good hands and there was no need for her to fly to California. I told her I was "at peace" whether I lived or died. This didn't please Mother. "I don't like the sound of your voice, Jimmy. It's got no fight in it," she said. I answered patiently, "That's because I'm *not* fighting, Mom." She shot back, "Well you damned well ought to be!" I ignored her. Mothers.

A researcher at Princeton University, all the way from across the continent, spotted the pattern of Motrin anaphylaxis. Apparently he specialized in it, and I was a classic case. The fact that I'd been taking a baby aspirin every day for a couple of years previously so as to avoid heart disease had not been enough to trigger my extreme allergy to aspirin. The Motrin put me over some biochemical threshold and, poof, I was on my way to glory. Now I wear a very expensive, rather handsome, medical alert bracelet that warns everybody not to give me any aspirin. I'm told that a single aspirin would likely cause a recurrence and that next time I'll never make it to a hospital. Fine. I'm not tempted to test the hypothesis.

After a couple of more weeks of recuperation in southern California and one more trip to the ER to get an adrenalin shot to my heart (recall that scene at the end of the movie *Pulp Fiction*), I was reborn. Like many other death survivors, I celebrate two birthdays now. According to the one in May 1951, I'm fifty-four years old. According to the other in September 1996, I'm nine. I prefer the latter, and I tend to act my age. Ask any of my friends.

6

White Man in 3-D
Death, Depression, and Divorce

Those of us born white, male, heterosexual, and in the U.S. middle class will never have to suffer certain things. Bigotry targeted at persons of color. Discrimination experienced by women. Fear and hatred aimed at gays. Indignity, insecurity, and ill health associated with poverty. To say nothing of what folks endure in certain parts of sub-Saharan Africa, *poblaciones* of Latin America, refugee camps in Pakistan, or political settlements in the Middle East. Our comparative lack of suffering is not an entitlement or even, necessarily, a blessing. It just is.

The worst stuff you're asked to suffer if you're born in the United States as a middle-class, white, heterosexual male all happens to begin with the letter "D." *Death. Depression. Divorce.*

Death, for me, did not constitute suffering. Not really (see the previous chapter). Depression, on the other hand, definitely does. It's neither fun nor interesting. It's definitely life-threatening, as well as life-quashing, life-debilitating, and life-sucking. So-called "chronic depression" won't go away, which is why it's called "chronic." I became aware of mine at age nineteen, although the condition may have predated that. When I say "aware," I don't mean that I had a word for it when I was nineteen. I simply mean that that was the first time I wanted to commit suicide, and I possessed no rational reason for doing so. I'd fallen into what William Styron describes quite rightly as "madness."

For many years, the symptoms of my depression were occasional anxiety attacks. (Again, I was unaware of this vocabulary.) For no apparent reason, I'd panic. My life felt like it was collapsing around me. I'd seek out a private space, usually dark, curl up on the floor, and cry uncontrollably. When my wife would happen upon me, I'd clutch her for dear life. The first couple of times this happened, she was sympathetic. She'd hold me, offering comfort. After that, however, she tired of what she perceived as my histrionics. "You're *so* theatrical," she'd say.

In my early forties, these occasional panic attacks began to occur more frequently until, at some point, they merged into an indistinguishable mass. Storm clouds moved into my psyche and stalled, forming a permanent, ominous weather condition. I didn't feel I could talk about this to anyone. Besides, one manifestation of the depression was pulling away from everyone else. The simplest interactions required inordinate energy. Going through a workday — and I never missed one — *exhausted* me.

Still, I did not use the word "depression." At the time, I knew people who were clinically depressed, including my older sister. It never occurred to me that I was ill. I simply fought against whatever it was that was getting me down. My wife consigned my attitudes and behavior to the adjective "weird." She'd given up.

Then I thought about suicide. I can't say whether my experience is typical of others who contemplate suicide. However, I'm guessing that it is different from what someone might imagine who has never considered the act. I made no dramatic decision to kill myself. It simply felt like the right next thing to do. It made sense, which, I later concluded, is proof positive of the madness of depression.

At that time, age forty-three, I felt that it would be better for my family — wife and two sons — if I weren't alive any longer. I felt I was a burden to them or, at least, a nuisance. I'm sure in many ways I *was* a burden and a nuisance, especially to my wife.

I was scheduled to make a trip to Chicago for a meeting of an advisory board to the Illinois Arts Council. I made this trip a few times each year, always by Amtrak from southern Illinois, and I decided on this particular weekend that I'd kill myself. My wife and sons were going to Indiana for the same weekend, to visit her parents. I thought I'd kill myself in Chicago, rather than at home, because then my family wouldn't have to clean up the mess, and my boys wouldn't be traumatized by finding their dead father. Again, all of this made perfectly good sense to me, and I approached the end casually. I felt no particular emotion.

I don't know the reason, but I visualize the abyss as being to my right.

I made the hotel reservation, but I just packed an overnight bag. I didn't bother with clothes for the entire weekend, and I didn't take along the files of proposals for the advisory board meeting. I wasn't going to attend.

Once in Chicago, I called my sister and asked to meet her at the restaurant of the Shedd Aquarium. We had a nice lunch, chit-chatted. Then she drove me back to the hotel, and it was time to do it. I was saved by a phone call from a friend. She'd gone to considerable trouble to find me, and it didn't seem polite to brush her off. I can't remember a single thing we talked about. Apparently she discerned that I was in a bad way, and she kept me on the phone *all night* talking, talking, talking.

My depression was diagnosed soon thereafter. I started to see a psychotherapist, and I began to take serotonin reuptake medications. (I still do.) Depression is a tough condition. One has no energy. One wants to sleep incessantly. In my case, I couldn't wait to get home from work and flop into bed. I had no trouble sleeping twelve, fourteen hours each night. I used to experience dizziness and, occasionally, pass out, necessitating three different ambulance trips to hospital emergency rooms.

For about five years, I walked along a very fine line separating life from death. I had no particular death wish. It's just that my days and nights were lived on the edge of an abyss. I don't know the reason, but I visualize the abyss as being to my right. Depression exhausted me, in part, because of living on the edge of this abyss. It took enormous energy to do even the simplest thing. I was always afraid that I might stumble one step to the right and fall over the edge. I tried to avoid falling over, mind you, but I couldn't move away from the edge. Every step forward had to be taken very carefully.

On the few more occasions when I had suicidal thoughts, the abyss became attractive. I learned to call my therapist immediately and, in due course, suicide disappeared from my thinking. I'm confident it'll never return.

Here's what Prozac — and its successors — does for me. It *doesn't* alter my mood. It *hasn't* changed my personality. It *doesn't* supercharge me or give me any feeling of well-being. Quite simply, the pharmaceutical miracle moves me about five steps to the left of the abyss. That's it. That's all. And it's everything.

The abyss is still there. I can see it. However, I'm no longer walking along its edge. I can move through my days with confidence because, even if I trip, I know I'm not going to stumble into the abyss. If, as rarely happens, I sense myself moving closer to the abyss, I call for help. Sometimes, my doctor changes dosage. The chemical balancing afforded by medication has this literal reference, in my case. It provides a psychological, almost physical, balancing. I walk on firm ground, several feet away from despair.

Depression, I think, qualifies as a kind of suffering. It's chronic and ongoing. One can't explain it, not adequately, to anyone else. It's utterly isolating. And it consumes all one's energy in order to cope with the pain.

Divorce — the third "D" experienced by white, male, middle-class, heterosexual, American men — constituted, for me, the most acute suffering. Not the longest lasting. Depression wins that distinction hands down. But divorce is the most anguishing, the most heart- and gut-wrenching. Everyone who's experienced divorce has his (or her) war stories, and I needn't detail mine to make my point. Instead, let me identify the distinctive categories of suffering that divorce entails.

First, divorce provokes "narrative instability." With the rupture of a married couple and the dissolution of their relationship, personal stories require revision. This is so for both spouses. It's so for the children. In varying degrees, it's the case for extended family members, in-laws, and friends, as well. For the spouses, though, divorce means losing narrative autonomy over one's own story. Competing stories that begin with "He" or "She" as told by the divorcing spouse begin to challenge and compete with the first-person narrator, "I," so long in command. This narrative contest, which may eventually get played out in a divorce courtroom, but which most certainly performs well through e-mails, over phone lines, and among friends, families, and colleagues, can be deeply hurtful to both parties. The pain is genuine and, often, prolonged. The attendant suffering is real and probably unprecedented in one's experience.

Second, when going through divorce, one invariably meets one's own Shadow, to borrow C. G. Jung's term — one's dark or hidden aspects. Self-doubt and recrimination are commonplace. Rock-bottom self-esteem is the norm. Manifestations may include sleeplessness, anxiety, physical ailments, lethargy, substance abuse, fits of rage, and so forth. Again, images associated with the divorcing man's Shadow self are familiar to everyone. As much a monster as the man may be portrayed in the alternative stories of a hurting wife, those monstrous projections probably don't compare to the ugly features of his own self-portrait. As with loss of narrative stability, the omnipresence of one's Shadow self creates conditions for genuine suffering.

With the rupture of a married couple and the dissolution of their relationship, personal stories require revision.

Third, when going through divorce, a man feels that he's "fallen short" in many regards. He has *fallen short* of vows uttered, promises made. He has *fallen short* of the expectations of parents, self, and society at large. Ultimately, he may feel that he has *fallen short* of the glory of God. Even the most rational, well-balanced guy is going to feel this sense of falling short. Others may feel cut off from grace, from love, from forgiveness. In short, they are damned.

*D*eath, *D*epression, and *D*ivorce are the three forms of suffering most widely available to white heterosexual men in the American middle class. None is pleasant. All are painful, to varying degrees. And, paradoxically, the three Ds are "a good thing," to quote the bromide of preimprisonment Martha Stewart. They're "a good thing" because, with any luck at all, they move a man along the spiritual alphabet toward *E*mpathy. I'm not sure that most white heterosexual men of the American middle class, lacking an opportunity to suffer, could experience empathy at all and, therefore, they would run the profound risk of being cut off from all other classifications of human being.

By suffering death, depression, or divorce, one can, if lucky, find empathy for the pain of others, pain that one may not experience personally — certain kinds of loss, prejudice, injustice, and so forth. The three Ds of a white man's suffering probably don't begin to yield empathy until middle age; their benefits accrue slowly. Hence, it's incumbent on white men to make the most of the latter part of their lives. Having by then experienced a bit of genuine suffering and thereby produced a modicum of empathy, one should put it to use in the making of *compassion*. This compassion, if achieved at all, will become manifest only after fifty.

If the logic of my argument is persuasive, I say to all white, heterosexual men of the American middle class, *Be thankful for Death, Depression, and Divorce.* They are the keys to your humanity. And I say to all women, persons of color, gays, lesbians, children, and poor folk, *Be thankful for any white man's Death, Depression, or Divorce,* because these are the experiences that will make him bearable and, just possibly, a positive contributor to society's good.

Now if you should meet a white, heterosexual, middle-class American male who's attained the age of fifty *without* experiencing death, depression, or divorce, do him, yourself, and society a big favor. I've outlined the three strategies for creating empathy and compassion in an otherwise obstinate form of human being. Implement them. First, try divorcing the guy. And if that doesn't work, try to create conditions yielding chronic depression. Remember: it must be chronic. Finally, as a last resort, shoot him. If the first two fail to create an empathic human being through genuine suffering, the third almost always works. That, or it will eliminate the problem altogether.

BIBLICAL
NARRATIVES

7

Vocation Education

I want to distinguish between two radically different approaches to making life choices — the professional and the vocational. The *professional* approach is so familiar as to be a cultural commonplace. It has such primacy in personal power, economic currency, and institutional warrant that it claims near monopoly status: Is there any other way to make a decision? This professional approach is based in logic and is susceptible to quantitative analysis.

Imagine a college undergraduate deciding whether or not to pursue a career in medicine (or law or accounting). Using a professional approach to making this choice, she might begin by considering its advantages and disadvantages. Under "Advantages," she lists the reasons to pursue a career in medicine — personal satisfaction, substantial income, social prestige. Under "Disadvantages," she lists the drawbacks — difficult training, job stress. If the list of advantages accumulates to a much longer length than the disadvantages, the logic of a professional approach is satisfied. Her parents and teachers will validate the sensibleness of her decision. It's *rational*.

Alternatively, this hypothetical student might calculate the odds of making it in the proposed profession. "Doing the odds" is another methodology of the professional approach to decision-making. "What are the odds that I'll make it into med school, or later, become board certified?" If the odds for success are high, then the decision is approved.

There's nothing wrong with this professional approach to decision-making. It's sensible. It receives such high societal endorsement as to raise the question whether any other approach is required.

Here's the rub.

Imagine a second college undergraduate who wants to become a novelist (or actor or cellist). He tries using the conventional predictors for successful decision-making. He eagerly lists as one "advantage" to becoming a novelist: "I really *want* to do it." Under "disadvantages," a longer list grows: unreliable income, no job security, publication is difficult. When this student does the odds, things look even worse. The odds against an unsolicited manuscript at a major New York publishing house are 18,000 to 1 — dubious as the basis for a major life choice. What's more, his parents or teachers are unlikely to support his choice. Responses range from the patronizing ("That would make a nice *hobby*") to the anxious ("How will you make a *living?*").

This second student needs a whole other logic than the professional approach to affirm his choice. How, then, does anyone choose against the odds, ignoring a long list of disadvantages, and still experience validation of his or her decision?

The odds against an unsolicited manu-script at a major New York publishing house are 18,000 to 1 — dubious as the basis for a major life choice.

"Vocation" represents a radical alternative to "profession." The two approaches cannot compete with each other because they do not occupy the same field of play. They're completely different, rooted in soils from different planets all together.

The word "vocation" derives from the Latin infinitive *vocare,* to call, carrying inside it the Latin noun *vox,* or voice. The simplest English translation of "vocation" is "calling." In common parlance, "vocation" and "profession" are sometimes used interchangeably. For my purposes, however, they must remain distinct because they are decidedly different. In the 1960s and 1970s, the word "vocation" was co-opted by a technical education movement, or "voc-tech" for short. This label usually meant instruction in auto mechanics, refrigeration, or electronic repairs. Again, for my purposes, one must strip such connotations from the Velcro surfaces of the word. I'm aiming at the *ancient* understanding of "vocation."

In Hebrew Scripture, Moses had a vocation. In Christian Scripture, Mary had a vocation. There is no profession called "Liberator of Slaves" and, if there were, the list of disadvantages to such a career choice would be much longer than the list of advantages. Likewise, there is no profession called "Mother of God." Again, if there were, the odds against success would be infinite. Neither Mary nor Moses subscribed to a professional approach when making their life-defining decisions. Each understood this alternative paradigm.

Recall the story of Moses, whether from its biblical text or from its Hollywood retelling in *The Ten Commandments*. Moses, a Jewish slave raised incognito in the home of the Egyptian pharaoh, struggled with his own identity. He experienced increasing empathy for his kin, the Hebrew slaves. One day, while he was walking in the desert, from the midst of a burning bush a voice called out: "Moses, set my people free." Moses recognized the

Speaker as the God of his people. And his first response was to offer a minor correction to God. "I believe you have my brother, Aaron, in mind for this job. He's the one who got straight A's in Public Speaking." Interestingly, this initial reaction of Moses represented a rational, professional approach to the life choice facing him. He encouraged God to compare résumés, his own versus Aaron's, believing that Aaron had a better chance of succeeding than did Moses, better *odds*. Notwithstanding, Moses was the one God had in mind after all, and Moses would have to choose whether or not to accept this calling on the basis of some logic other than career planning.

Mary, a mere teenager, faced a similar dilemma when called by an angel of God to bear a child by the Holy Spirit. Mary didn't ask for this assignment. She never typed "Mother of God" at the top of a résumé after "Career Objective." For Mary to pursue this destiny as a career option, rather than accepting it as her vocation, would have been presumptuous in the extreme, even blasphemous. To say yes, Mary had to invoke the logic of vocation, not profession.

Common to every story of vocation within the biblical traditions, both Hebrew and Christian, are four characteristics. First, a person is called *for a special purpose,* Moses to lead his people from captivity to the Promised Land, Mary to give birth to God's son. Accepting a call means committing to its fulfillment.

Second, the person who is called has a *special gift*. This should not be confused with aptitude, skill set, or talent. A special gift associated with vocation must be revealed to the individual.

Third, implicit to vocation is the presence of a *Caller.* In biblical narratives, the Caller has a name — Yahweh, God, Jesus. The Caller's voice is heard as something outside the person called.

Fourth, accepting a vocation leads to *a life of sacrifice, faith, and, often, darkness.* Neither Moses nor Mary could have predicted what answering the call would mean. Each had to sacrifice other life possibilities in order to say yes to the Caller. Each had to exercise faith in order to accept the unknown, to walk into darkness in order to find the light.

Vocation focuses on obedience, accountability, and faithfulness to the Caller. Vocation demands life-ordering disciplines to ensure responsiveness, requiring silence in order to be attentive to the Other.

Discerning one's vocation relies on a process quite different from choosing a profession. A vocation must be heard or felt with passion. This passion — to write, to paint, to heal, to teach — must be confirmed first by oneself. Second, it needs to match one's *gifts*. And, finally, it needs to be confirmed by a *community of others* or by a *mentor.* This final step helps preclude mistaking a personal compulsion with a genuine vocation.

Elizabeth O'Connor wrote insightfully of vocation from a religious perspective:

> *If I develop one gift, it means that other gifts will not be used. Doors will close on a million lovely possibilities. I will become a painter or a doctor only if denial becomes a part of my picture of reality. Commitment at the point of my gifts means that I must give up being a straddler. Somewhere in the deeps of me I know this.... My commitment will give me an identity. When asked who I am, I will be reminded that the answer lies in the exercise of my gifts.* *

Almost all the support systems for personal development in U.S. society favor a professional approach to decision-making over a vocational approach. Formal education — beginning at least with high school and continuing through college with its near-exclusive emphasis on career planning — can hardly recognize anything *other* than the professional paradigm.

My own *profession* is higher education; I am a professor and a dean. However, my *vocation* is writing; I

---

*Elizabeth O'Connor, *Eighth Day of Creation: Gifts and Creativity* (Waco, Tex.: Word Books, 1971), 42–43.

am a novelist. I bootleg my vocation through my profession as, frankly, most artists have done throughout Western history. As an educator who orders his personal life according to vocation, I worry that university life provides scant vocabulary for discussing vocation. I worry that the perceived urgency to build a student's résumé leaves too little time for silence, for listening to the still, small voice of the Caller. I worry that all parties to the educational enterprise (students, parents, and teachers) have come to expect too little for their tuition and their time.

As a college dean, when I speak to incoming freshmen and their parents, I say, "Please expect more of this institution than merely whether you will obtain an entry-level job when you graduate. To place the bar there is to place it too low. While an undergraduate, experiment rigorously and radically to discover your God-given gifts. Develop the spiritual discipline and emotional maturity to go on 'internal retreat,' listening for the Voice of a Caller, hearing the possibilities of Vocation. Turn your focus from the want ads to your own wants, and to the wants of your Creator. Anything less is not worthy of the name *higher* education."

Rainer Maria Rilke, the wonderful German poet, in the volume *Letters to a Young Poet* wrote what could be a primer on vocational thinking:

Nobody can counsel and help you, nobody. There is only one single way. Go into yourself. Search for the reason that bids you write; find out whether it is spreading out its roots in the deepest places of your heart, acknowledge to yourself whether you would have to die if it were denied you to write. This above all — ask yourself in the stillest hour of your night: Must I write? Delve into yourself for a deep answer. And if this should be affirmative, if you may meet this earnest question with a strong and simple "I must," then build your life according to this necessity: your life even into its most indifferent and slightest hour must be a sign of this urge and a testimony to it.*

There is nothing wrong with the professional approach to making major life choices. It's just not sufficient. Vocation offers a radical alternative, and a more ancient approach. Professional thinking may be necessary to ensure economic success. Vocational thinking is necessary to ensure personal fulfillment. To extrapolate from Elizabeth O'Connor: *Not* to use one's gifts, regardless of excuse, is to live an anguished life apart from creativity. Look around and see if it isn't true.

---

*Translation by M. D. Herter Norton, Norton Library edition (New York: Norton, 1954), 18–19.

8

Moses, Hezekiah, and Yale's Gang of Four

In literary study, most critical discussion boils down to one question: Who, finally, has the authority to say what a text means? Must one consult the *author's intention* and, if so, how should this be discerned? Can one rely upon an individual *reader's interpretation* of the text as being right for him or her? Or, by some independent laws of criticism, can the *text in itself* (*das Ding an sich*) serve as a reliable guide to its own understanding?

These questions report rather simply a crux of criticism that was argued in the treatises of ancient Greeks and remains central to the theories of contemporary critics (one school ignobly dubbed Yale's "Gang of Four": J. Hillis Miller, Paul de Man, Harold Bloom, and Geoffrey Hartman). The question of who can be trusted to interpret a text — whether the author, the reader, or the language itself — cannot, I think, be answered with any certainty, and this is to the good. Rather, one's answer to the question usually reflects some conscious, intuitive, or inherited philosophy of interpretation and language. My own perspective demands a drawing together of writer, reader, and text into a contractual union, an implied covenant.

I began thinking seriously about the links among writer, reader, and text when recently I reread the Old Testament account of snakebites, Moses, and the serpent of bronze. I had thought before about the issue of interpretive authority and stand in awe of Flannery O'Connor's sacramental view, as well as Wolfgang Iser's explanation of the reading process in his books *The Implied Reader* and *The Act of Reading*. But it was that bronze serpent, Moses, and especially Hezekiah that brought the matter into clearer focus.

The short story, anthologized in Numbers 21, is familiar:

> *The people came to Moses and said, "We sinned when we spoke against the Lord and you. Plead with the Lord to rid us of the snakes." Moses therefore pleaded with the Lord for the people; and the Lord told Moses to make a serpent of bronze and erect it as a standard, so that anyone who had been bitten could look at it and recover. So Moses made a bronze serpent and*

erected it as a standard, so that when a snake had bit-
ten a man, he could look at the bronze serpent and
recover. (NEB)

This anecdote is straightforward and characteristically brief. Even if the story ended here, the biblical tale could serve as an exemplum of one artistic symbol and how it worked. The serpent of bronze crafted by Moses was "erected as a standard," an artifact depicted in picture and film as a snake coiled on a staff. We do not know what kind of craftsman Moses was, but we may assume that he fashioned a suitable serpent-likeness. And when a snake-bit victim looked at this bronze sculpture, he or she recovered. It was a gracious artistic experience, a miracle of intention and perception.

The serpent of bronze was a special kind of symbol that made visible an implied covenant between Yahweh and the people: "If you look on this man-made object with faith, you will experience divine healing." Moses' part in this transaction was that of an intermediary, a priest handling the mundane materials of a sacrament. Moses, as artist, followed a divine impulse, sculpted the snake, and offered it for the healing of those who would receive. The covenant's power resided entirely in a transaction between Yahweh and the people; yet Moses alone could be seen to *do* anything.

It would be possible to argue from this story a certain view of the reading process. A text stands, as did the serpent of bronze, in testament to the author's creative impulse. His or her task is to fashion this vision in such a way that others, too, may see and enter into the created world. The validity of an artist's vision and of the finished work can be measured only in terms of transformations in the reader's life, and these depend partly upon what the reader brings to the experience, upon his or her modicum of faith. Given this view, the authority of a created text draws upon an implied covenant between writer and reader, a contract made visible in the text.

Because an artist's creative impulse remains a mystery, and the reader's process of perception is equally impenetrable, it may be tempting to accord an independent power to the text itself. Language, at least, does not change. The permanence of print adds to the illusion of solid reality, analyzable. As appealing and useful as this view may be, the notion of a self-contained text providing all the necessary evidence for its proper interpretation has proven insufficient to literary critics and was utterly blasphemous to the ancient Hebrews. Several hundred years after the desert incidents of snakebite and healing, the Old Testament says, came a sequel to that story (see 2 Kings 18):

In the third year of Hoshea son of Elah king of Israel, Hezekiah son of Ahaz king of Judah became king. He was twenty-five years old when he came to the throne, and he reigned in Jerusalem for twenty-nine years; his mother was Abi daughter of Zechariah. He did what was right in the eyes of the Lord, as David his forefather had done. It was he who suppressed the hill shrines, smashed the sacred pillars, cut down every sacred pole and broke up the bronze serpent that Moses had made; for up to that time the Israelites had been burning sacrifices to it; they called it Nehushtan. (NEB)

This description of Hezekiah's reign is, to me, fascinating. The people of Israel had ceased to view the bronze serpent as a covenant symbol and had begun to see it as a powerful thing in itself: they named it and offered sacrifices to it. What had been a token of grace became an idol. Hezekiah distinguished himself by breaking up the sculpture. The object was destroyed in the same way it was created — by an impulse to obey on the part of Hezekiah. Anyone who has read the two volumes of Kings and has suffered through the despairing history of monarchs "who did what was wrong in the eyes of the Lord" will appreciate the magnitude of Hezekiah's act. The serpent of bronze offered healing both in its making and in its unmaking. Its meaning resided always in the intention of Yahweh and only by covenantal extension in the hands of Moses, Hezekiah, and the people.

I believe that the lesson for a writer in this two-part biblical story is a warning that artistic power and interpretive authority are shared phenomena. An author plays his or her part, the reader takes on an active role, and the text itself is essential to the engagement between writer and reader. The three are linked in a covenant relationship. But the validity of that union, while depending upon the contribution of each participant, is guaranteed by an outside power, present and invisible. This mystical view increases the author's and reader's accountabilities: one is held responsible not only for a proper viewing of the art object (the text) but also for its relation to an external reality, to a life outside itself.

What had been a token of grace became an idol. Hezekiah distinguished himself by breaking up the sculpture.

For those who share this sense of an implied covenant in the reading process, a writer's intention alone cannot serve to authorize meaning. Reader perception alone cannot validate an artistic experience. Even the text cannot enjoy complete autonomy. All are contracted into a union. And, for the writer or reader with a Christian perspective, this union is experienced as a covenant of grace. The ultimate validity of a created text is its efficacy as a felt token of the Creator's impulse.

9

Let's Not Lose Our Heads

Herod was the one who had John arrested and bound in prison on account of Herodias, the wife of his brother Philip, whom he had married. John had said to Herod, "It is not lawful for you to have your brother's wife." Herodias harbored a grudge against him and wanted to kill him but was unable to do so. Herod feared John, knowing him to be a righteous and holy man, and kept him in custody. When he heard him speak he was very much perplexed, yet he liked to listen to him. She had an opportunity one day when Herod, on his birthday, gave a banquet for his courtiers, his military officers, and the leading men of Galilee. Herodias's own daughter came in and performed a dance that delighted Herod and his guests. The king said to the girl, "Ask of me whatever you wish and I will grant it to you." He even swore to her, "I will grant you whatever you ask of me, even to half of my kingdom." She went out and said to her mother, "What shall I ask for?" She replied, "The head of John the Baptist." The girl hurried back

*to the king's presence and made her request, "I want
you to give me at once on a platter the head of John the
Baptist." The king was deeply distressed, but because of
his oaths and the guests he did not wish to break his
word to her. So he promptly dispatched an executioner
with orders to bring back his head. He went off and
beheaded him in the prison. He brought in the head
on a platter and gave it to the girl. The girl in turn
gave it to her mother. When his disciples heard about
it, they came and took his body and laid it in a tomb.*

Mark 6:17–29 (NAB)

Well, this Gospel story gives me the creeps. That may
sound blasphemous, but it's the truth. It's my privilege
once each year, when my pastor is on vacation during
July, to preach a homily. I'm always hopeful that the
lectionary readings will turn up something about joy,
because that's a subject I'd like to preach on. Joy seems
to be the forgotten theological virtue, overshadowed by
faith, hope, and charity, even though true joy, whenever I see it in evidence, is one of the surest signs of
God's presence in a person's life, and it draws me like
a magnet. One need hardly say, there ain't no joy in
the story of John's beheading, unless you were to tell it
from Herodias's point of view, which I have no intention of doing. Perhaps next year I'll get lucky and draw

a joyful text. Also, I dream of preaching on Pentecost Sunday because I think those tongues of fire are just about the coolest special effect in all of church history, and I'd like to contemplate Pentecost from the listeners' point of view (that is, as a miracle of perception rather than performance, each one hearing in a different language). Fat chance a layman is going to get to preach on Pentecost Sunday.

My pastor sent me the lectionary readings in a gray envelope, which proved appropriate, and I was excited a couple of weeks ago to open it up and see what the readings would be. Can you imagine drawing a shorter straw than the beheading of John the Baptist! I must confess that I do not go to scary movies, I do not read Stephen King, and I didn't make it all the way through the film version of *The Wizard of Oz* until I'd reached adulthood. I do not truck with violence. I do not like blood and gore. It would have been all right with me if the story of John's beheading had not made the final cut into the New Testament, saving me from several nightmares in a Baptist boyhood and from a disagreeable sermon topic today. By the way, apparently, Herod had second thoughts about this story, too, even though he was the one who caused it. Our Gospel reading opens with King Herod's interpretation of who Jesus was. Herod was convinced, after hearing stories of Jesus' miraculous powers, that Jesus must be John the Baptist, whom Herod had beheaded, returned to life, and this probably made Herod very nervous.

Well, fact is, the story of John's beheading did make the final cut, and not just in Mark's Gospel. Hence, as believers, as followers of Christ, even as one who covers his eyes at scary movies and prefers not to think of the image of Miss Gulch riding her bicycle with Toto in the basket, we've got to deal with this R-rated story.

John the Baptist and Jesus were very close. Their mothers, Elizabeth and Mary, were cousins; hence, the boys were second cousins. John devoted his life to preparing a way for the Lord, following a prophet's vocation, living an ascetic life of deprivation, preaching repentance, baptizing believers, including the familiar scene of his baptizing Jesus himself, although John, you'll recall, protested that it was Jesus who should have baptized him, not the other way around.

There could not have been a more loyal devotee of our Lord than John the Baptist. He was not one of the Twelve, not an apostle. He was a precursor of Jesus, the one who went before. And Jesus at one point preaches to a crowd about John the Baptist, praising him as a great prophet, reserving words of commendation for John that Jesus never used for any of his disciples. You'll find this honorific sermon in the eleventh chapter of

Matthew. Another evidence of Jesus' affection for John the Baptist is that when news comes to him of John's death, we learn from Matthew (not from our writer, Mark) that Jesus withdrew in a boat to a deserted place to grieve. It was one of those many instances in the Gospels when crowds followed Jesus, and he, moved by compassion, gave up his solitude to heal the sick and to preach.

There's an earlier prison episode to John the Baptist's story before the horrific tale of our Gospel reading today. It's not recorded in Mark but in Matthew. John is in prison and hears of the works of Jesus. So he sends his disciples to Jesus with this question, "Are you the one who is to come, or should we look for another?" Now, doesn't that strike you as a peculiar question for John to ask? Really, a very peculiar question. For goodness' sake, John has been preaching for several years that Jesus *is* the Messiah, that Jesus *is* the one. He probably grew up believing that his second cousin Jesus was the one because his mother, Elizabeth, certainly believed that Mary was carrying the son of God when the two pregnant cousins met before either gave birth. John baptized Jesus and saw the heavens open up and the spirit descend on Jesus in the form of a dove, hearing the divine pronouncement: "This is my son in whom I am well pleased." John knew who Jesus was. And yet, imprisoned, he sends his disciples to Jesus to find out "Are you the one, or should we look for another?"

Recall that our Lord doesn't chastise John. He shows no impatience. Instead, Jesus tells John's disciples, "Go back and tell John what you hear and see: the blind regain their sight, the lame walk, lepers are cleansed, the deaf hear, the dead are raised, and the poor have the good news proclaimed to them. And blessed is the one who takes no offense at me." It's immediately after sending John's disciples back to him that Jesus delivers his sermon in praise of John the Baptist.

I identify with John the Baptist in this first prison story. Its theme is so familiar to us Christians: I believe, Lord, but help Thou my unbelief. That's me all over as a Christian. Yes, I believe. But I need help with my *un*belief.

I have never been in prison myself. In fact, it is one of the less noble goals of my life to try, if I can, to stay out of prison. If I were a better Christian, one who stood up against injustice, who fought systemic evil, who trespassed against unfair laws, I'd probably spend weeks, months, or years in prison. But I don't aspire to this. My own father did time in federal prison, though not for any crime of conscience, and my visits to him many years ago persuaded me it would be an unpleasant place to live. I developed an early aversion to prison life and haven't matured beyond that spiritual allergy.

The closest I'm likely to come to John the Baptist's temporary loss of faith, probably occasioned by the uncomfortable conditions of his prison life, is (as I mentioned earlier) clinical depression, a more or less permanent condition to which I've been sentenced since my teenage years and one that bears some analogy to imprisonment, complete with bouts of solitary confinement, deprivation of light, and severe restrictions on freedom. When one is depressed, belief presents special challenges, just as prison occasioned John the Baptist to ask our Lord, "Are you the one?" And do you know what Jesus' loving response, his tender response, teaches me? That the question is okay to ask. The question itself — Are you the one? — is *not* a denial of faith; it's a stage of faith; it's a step of faith; it's a part of faith. By our asking the question honestly, humbly, our Lord has opportunity to answer with quiet assurance: "Open your eyes. Open your ears. Look. Listen. There is healing. Vision is restored. The poor receive good news." And what the biblical text need not say, because it is self-evident in the story of John the Baptist, and it is reminiscent of our own Christian experience, is this: when we look around ourselves, when we listen, then our faith is restored and belief deepens.

So now we get to the denouement of poor old John the Baptist, whose earthly life ends like some kind of perverse practical joke. He's a victim of petty jealousies and palace politics. How often the heroes of our faith do not get to end their stories in triumph. Moses, after all he does for the children of Israel, does not get to enter with them into the Promised Land. Every single disciple, with the exception of Judas and possibly John — another John now, not John the Baptist — was executed. The plot details of the deaths of Christian martyrs leave the best horror writers in the dust. So it was with John the Baptist. His disciples come to Herod, ask for the body, and offer the respect of a proper burial — just as our Christian community ritualizes the passage of each and every member with a memorial service commemorating a life of faith and looking forward to an eternity of joy.

I don't think the church elders in their wisdom included the tale of John's beheading in today's lectionary as either a cautionary tale or an exemplar. I think the story, for all its gruesomeness, is there to say that the ultimate meaning of a Christian narrative, of a Christian's pilgrimage, is not so much in the plot details, and certainly not in those over which one has no control. The ultimate meaning of a Christian narrative, of a Christian's pilgrimage, is in *character and theme*. We bring what faith we can to the moments of our lives, and when that faith falters, we send out an SOS, "Are You the one?" to which Our Lord always responds, "It is I, the Alpha and Omega, Beginning and End, the same yesterday, today, and forever. You are my beloved brother. You are my beloved sister. In you I am well pleased."

And with that assurance, bring on whatever plot line you will, even if it involves a dance with seven veils, because God is with us.

10

We Are People of Gospel Imagination

Jesus proposed another parable to them. "The kingdom of heaven may be likened to a man who sowed good seed in his field. While everyone was asleep his enemy came and sowed weeds all through the wheat, and then went off. When the crop grew and bore fruit, the weeds appeared as well. The slaves of the householder came to him and said, 'Master, did you not sow good seed in your field? Where have the weeds come from?' He answered, 'An enemy has done this.' His slaves said to him, 'Do you want us to go and pull them up?' He replied, 'No, if you pull up the weeds you might uproot the wheat along with them. Let them grow together until harvest; then at harvest time I will say to the harvesters, "First collect the weeds and tie them in bundles for burning; but gather the wheat into my barn." ' "

Matthew 13:24–30 (NAB)

This Gospel story is so familiar and, at the same time, so paradoxical, so enigmatic. It fits into that hefty anthology of parables Jesus told about seeds and planting and farmers. Remember the Gospel story about the farmer who sowed seed on three different kinds of soil. And there are the stories of separating wheat from chaff, or mustering the faith to move a mountain with the latent power of a tiny seed. It's interesting that Jesus himself, so far as we know, was not a farmer. He was a carpenter. And the preponderance of his disciples were fishermen. Nonetheless, these agricultural stories apply to everybody. We grasp their earthiness because they're rooted in common experience. This agricultural parable baffles me, scares me a bit too, because like so many of Jesus' stories, this one is challenging, even subversive.

A farmer sowed good seed for a wheat crop. When everybody was asleep — and sometimes this is a biblical code for folks not paying attention, not being watchful — an enemy came and planted weeds among the wheat. So we've got a planted field with a surprise waiting to sprout up. Sure enough, when the plants came up and bore grain, there came the nasty weeds as well. The farmer's staff made a report and asked the farmer whether he hadn't, perhaps, sowed some bad seed, inasmuch as there were so many weeds. And the farmer somehow knew, "Nope, this is the work of an enemy." His workers then suggested, "Well, why don't we just go out into the field and pull up all those weeds?" Which, I might add, sounds like a pretty sensible suggestion to me. But the farmer does not agree. Instead, he says, "If you start pulling up the weeds, you'll uproot some of the good wheat along with them, and I don't want that. Just let them both grow up together, the wheat and the weeds. At harvest time, we'll collect the weeds first, bind 'em up, and burn 'em. That'll leave all the good wheat, which we'll bundle together and put into my barn."

Okay, that's the story in a nutshell. It's an easy story. It's a memorable story. You can repeat it without too much risk of getting the gist wrong, or even forgetting any of the details. This is one of the things that I, as a writer, marvel at in Jesus' parables. They're such efficient narratives. They were always told out loud. There were no scribes writing them down, not that we're aware of. But you didn't need a scribe or a tape recorder or a videocam. The stories themselves are beautifully crafted, exquisitely memorable. You can easily imagine going home after a teaching day amid the hillside audience of Jesus and being able to repeat, almost verbatim, his stories at your dinner table. I happen to believe that many of his parables are very funny, though not particularly this one, and that their humor added to their memorability without subtracting from their significance. We'll save that point for another day when we try to squeeze a camel through the eye of a needle.

It's a memorable story. You can repeat it without too much risk of getting the gist wrong, or even forgetting any of the details.

As simple as the story itself is of the wheat and the weeds, its interpretation, its meaning, is tricky. It certainly appears to have eluded the disciples, and these fellows were not dumb. As often happens, after the crowd disperses, the disciples ask Jesus to return to a story, and they ask for the CliffsNotes. When Jesus had left the crowds and gone into a house, the disciples asked him, "Would you please explain to us the parable of the weeds in the field." And Jesus answered like a good middle-school teacher, not like a college professor. Instead of making his parable sound highfalutin and dependent on some abstract theory or theology, he explained it as clearly as could be, using a bunch of equal signs:

The farmer = the Son of Man

The field = the world

The good seed = the children of the kingdom

The weeds = the children of the evil one

The enemy who sowed the weeds = the devil

The harvest = the end of the age

The reapers of the harvest = angels

The idea of collecting up the weeds and burning them = what it's gonna be like at the end of the age for the children of the evil one. It's gonna be pretty bad with a furnace of fire, weeping, and gnashing of teeth. (Here Jesus extrapolates a bit beyond the original parable.)

And, finally, the good wheat = the righteous ones, who will shine like the sun in the kingdom of their Father.

You really couldn't ask for a clearer interpretive formula. Jesus closes this tutorial with his disciples by saying, "Let anyone with ears listen!" Apparently, St. Matthew went one better and took notes, either then or later.

Now let's think a minute about this simple story and this clear interpretation in terms of what it could possibly have meant in Jesus' time, and what it might mean for us today, for those of us who try to take Jesus' teachings, his life and example, seriously in our own lives and thinking.

One interpretation by biblical scholars who know a lot about the early church is that this story warns against constructing boundaries to ensure a "pure" community. In other words, there was apparently an impulse among some early Christians to define pretty clearly who was in and who was out. They kept wanting to add membership rules in order to keep their community "pure." And there were other Christians, including Matthew, who reminded them of this story by Jesus: don't be trying to exclude people. Instead, take whatever risks may be involved with inclusiveness, by accepting more people. Besides, as Jesus' story says at the end, it's not really our business to say who's in and who's out. That's up to God and the angels at the time of harvest, at the end of the age. We really don't have to worry about that. In this sense, the story reminds us of an earlier admonition by St. Matthew: "Judge not, lest ye be judged." (That's back in the seventh chapter, first verse.)

A more contemporary interpretation one can read among biblical scholars goes something like this: Let's not be shocked to find that in the world, in our own families, and even in the church, there's much good, but there's also much that isn't so good. There's occasional cruelty. People, including friends and family members, can cause deep pain as well as great joy. The church can be courageous at one moment and petty, even faithless, in the next. Bad mixes in with the good, and we ask, "Where did these weeds come from?"

When the farmer forbids his workers to go out into the field and pull the weeds, he's not calling for passivity in the face of evil. We can't interpret this to ignore injustice in the world, violence in our society, or wrong in the church. It seems to be a simple reminder of the way things are. We don't have the ability to get rid of all the weeds, and sometimes our efforts to pluck out the weeds can cause more harm then good. And, considering the end of the parable, there's obvious reason for hope. The weeds will ultimately be destroyed. Evil is temporary; good endures. We live in an imperfect world, and we are ourselves imperfect. No human effort will change that fact. Anyway, perfection isn't our job. Trying to be good, trying to live faithfully, confident in the eventual harvest, that's our job.

So, now let me try a little of my own interpretation, which you can take or leave, because I'm just a story writer.

The first question I have when listening to this parable is: Where am I located in the story? I suppose it's commonplace for listeners or readers to identify with the good wheat, or maybe with the workers who help the farmer. Well, the first thing I tell myself when hearing this story is: Try not to be one of the weeds. Check yourself from time to time and be sure you look like wheat, that you're growing up toward the sun, that you're producing some grain, and that you aren't reaching over and choking out the seedlings next to you.

And then the next thing for me — after I'm satisfied that I'm wheat and not weed — is to wonder how many applications there may be for this lesson to "let the weeds alone until the time for God's harvest."

Does this lesson apply to neighbors whose behavior clearly doesn't comport with the condo guidelines or, for that matter, with the commonsense norms of any civilized neighborhood? I wonder if I should keep my mouth shut?

Does this lesson apply at the workplace? Should I never be a whistleblower when I'm witness to evil, or illegal, behavior on the part of others?

Does this lesson have anything to do with a country's foreign policy? Should a nation not defend itself from evildoers, name the darned weeds, and yank 'em out?

Could we afford to wait for God's judgment at the end of time? Is that even prudent?

We could go on much further with a list of possible applications and difficult questions. I do not have answers to all these questions for myself. And when I do have answers for myself, I have no confidence that they would be right for you.

Let me close with one final idea, tied to the title I've given to this essay: "We Are People of Gospel Imagination."

There is one thing we can say when taking Jesus' stories, his teaching, to heart, and especially when we ponder the challenges of this commonplace story about the wheat and the weeds: the Gospel of Jesus Christ is an alternative way of seeing the world. It's not just a new pair of lenses by which to see the same old things. The Gospel gives us a whole new set of eyes, eyes that are transplanted with the sacred imagination of our Lord.

We can be light to the world, salt to the earth, only if we represent a different way of seeing things, a new way of being. The Gospel Imagination, to which Jesus' stories train us, is anathema to "conventional wisdom." The Gospel Imagination, to which we are called when we "put on the mind of Christ," cannot be measured by approval ratings or majority rules.

Seeing the world as Jesus saw it, and as Jesus invites us to see it, means seeing it with new eyes, smelling it with a new nose, tasting it in new flavors and seasonings, hearing it at wavelengths heretofore inaudible.

That's what Jesus' fantastic stories help us to do — to train our Gospel Imaginations. That's what his miracles challenge us to see — the scope and possibility of our Gospel Imaginations. And if his divine life and teaching is not sufficient for this training, he gives us one other helper. He says, in effect, if you would enter the Kingdom of Heaven, if you would put on the mind of Christ, if you would be possessed of the Gospel Imagination, become as one of these, a little child.

LANGUAGE
and
THEOLOGY

11

The Medium Is the Message
A View of the Incarnation

We in the church of today are in a better position to understand the Incarnation than were any of our predecessors in the Christian faith because of our awareness of media. One may think that the media have little or nothing to do with an understanding of the Gospel, but I am coming to believe that the notion of a medium has everything to do with my understanding of who Christ was as a man.

The word "medium" is used loosely today. We tend to associate it primarily with modern electronic media — television, film, radio. And these are important media, but they are by no means the only media by which we experience life. In fact, a medium may be any extension of the human body, doing the body's work. Marshall McLuhan tells us that the wheel is a medium — an extension of the foot. Clothing is an extension of the temperature-control system of the skin. Mirrors, cameras, and telescopes extend the eye.

The history of humanity can be read as a chronicle of new media, each altering the human environment and humanity itself. For instance, the alphabet was one of the first communications media to change human existence. Prior to its general use, one had to rely on memory to a degree incomprehensible to us today. With the alphabet, that was no longer necessary. People then could write what they wanted to remember, thus extending the mind's capability through the medium of the alphabet.

Hundreds of years later, another medium was invented, this one to assist the hand and the eye. It changed not only the course of history but of rational thought processes as well. This was Gutenberg's invention of movable type — the medium of print. We became a visually oriented people giving more credence to what is in print than to what is heard. With the widespread use of print, it was only what a person affixed a signature to that was binding — contracts, treaties and other written agreements.

The medium of print gave supremacy to the notion of order. Print is sequential. One letter follows another in an orderly fashion. One word follows another to make a sentence. We read, understand, and, it seems, even think from left to right in a linear manner. Much of what we call Western logic comes from the medium of print. One says, "That doesn't follow," meaning: "What you have said isn't true because it isn't linear." The medium itself is the message. It has controlled the way we think.

All of that is now changing with the advent of new electronic media, which demand an aural rather than a visual orientation. Sounds bombard us from all sides simultaneously, unlike the linear, one-at-a-time nature of sight (i.e., focusing). Our patterns of thought are changing as a result. We live by media and define ourselves in terms of the media we use.

We became a visually oriented people giving more credence to what is in print than to what is heard.

Consider the copying machine. It has made everyone his or her own publisher. It has dictated the structures of committees. It is the servant (or master?) of modern business administration. It has in effect invalidated all copyright laws. Another medium, the telephone, has shrunk time and space and has greatly altered the antique craft of letter-writing. Or consider two of the most popular media today: TV and film. Television is immanent light. When we turn on the box, light magically appears, and a disembodied voice addresses us. We listen — we have to. From the beginning of time, human beings have assumed that whenever there is immanent light and disembodied voice, God is speaking: the burning bush and Moses. The voice out of the whirlwind that spoke to Job. The voice of truth. The voice of God. The television. (Robbed of his Old Testament mode of communication, how would God speak to Moses today?)

Film, unlike television, is reflected light from a projector at the rear of the theater. It is somehow less credible than the immanent light of TV. But the cinema compensates by providing a macro-image of humanity. Human as hero, ten feet tall. We gladly sit back and look up to these heroes. In fact, we worship them as stars.

All of which is to say: Finally, in the 1960s and 1970s, we are beginning to understand the effects of media. We understand that the Vietnam war would have been different if there had been no television. We understand that the sexy girl or guy selling the product on TV is hitting our sales resistance below the level of consciousness. And we are beginning to understand the more subtle ways media control our lives.

We, as media consumers, as students of the media, are in a unique position to understand the Gospel because its focal point is wrapped up in what we have been calling a medium. The Word became flesh. Spirit became flesh. God became human — the Incarnation, a mixed medium. Jesus himself is a medium, an extension of God. The very fact that God the Spirit transforms into another medium, into the *medium* of the human body, is the message of the Gospel. John writes: "And the Word [which is itself a medium metaphor] was made flesh and dwelt among us, and we beheld his glory, the glory as of the only begotten of the Father, full of grace and truth."

The medium is the message. God cared so much for humankind as to transform spirit into a human being so that we could behold God more clearly, so that we could understand God better, so that we could more fully respond to God as Spirit.

Throughout church history we have devoted most of our attention and study to the content of the Gospel, to the words of Jesus, and this has been a proper commitment. But today we are in a better position than the church has ever been in before to understand the Incarnation as the Grand Miracle, as C. S. Lewis called it — the grand act of love and commitment on the part of God. It is to the medium that we respond.

I believe that our modern understanding of a medium has called to the fore the meaning of the Incarnation. We have a responsibility, it would seem, to our culture and society to interpret intelligently and to reembody within our own lives the meaning of Christ's Incarnation.

12

The Word Became Flesh, Then Digital

"And the Word became flesh." For two millennia and for countless generations, the church has celebrated Incarnation.

Now the word has become digital. At the turn of a millennium and for the first generation, this same church has the capacity to build community that is literally, not just metaphorically, universal, worldwide, spanning time and shrinking space.

What the prophets of old spoke is made manifest today in the pixeled print of a computer screen. Whether this second advent crashes into a babel of incoherence or descends as tongues of fire will depend more on the discernment of believers than on the technology of engineers.

The church's response to this second advent — the word become digital — should be nothing less than a joyous affirmation of the first. Technology extends Incarnation; it does not negate it.

When an eighty-nine-year-old grandmother sends daily e-mails to her ten grandchildren — all of them busy with important careers across three continents — she isn't lamenting a family's diaspora. She's reclaiming their familial bonds.

When senior citizens enroll in an electronic chat room to discuss public policy, they aren't isolating themselves from social engagement. They're transforming cultural politics.

When a virtual classroom links scholars in Tel Aviv with students in South Orange, New Jersey, this is not an example of "distanced learning." It's an experience of intimate connectedness.

From the beginning of narrative time, God has taken delight in what Marshall McLuhan used to call media, what Bill Gates still calls technology, and what the church has always called sacrament. Today, because of new communications technologies, flesh is becoming word. The sacrament of Incarnation proves reversible — and it's no less efficacious in making the about-face. The World Wide Web can shrink time and space into a single moment. The electronic beep of a computer may not sound as resonant as an Angelus bell, but it signals the same possibility of Incarnation.

Christian discernment should understand this because salvation itself depends on time and space merging into a single moment of grace.

Think of some commonplace figures of speech by which believers promise community to one another:

"I'll always be there for you."

"You can call on me anytime, day or night."

"I share your pain; I join your struggle."

Such assurances echo the resurrection words of Jesus to his disciples, anticipating the coming of the Holy Spirit. They also literalize the potential of the Internet.

Today, because of new communications technologies, flesh is becoming word.

I'm not arguing that technology is sacred in and of itself, any more than you could argue that human flesh, by itself, is more important than the dust to which it so quickly returns. The *word made flesh* and the *word made digital* are potentially sacred. They're sacraments. Both offer the possibility of divine connectedness between the Creator and the created, intimately linking person to person.

God continues to delight in the mystery of transformation. Incarnation is God's middle name, for goodness' sake. As today's body of Christ, the church should embrace technology. The personal computer can stroll right through the locked doors and closed borders of our communal life to announce, "Fear not. I am alive. The word has become digital and dwells among us."

I truly believe that our loving Lord is booting us up, gently, to get online and proclaim, "In the beginning was the Word." And the word goes on.

13

Language as Sacrament

[*Following an incident at Seton Hall University in which racist graffiti were printed on the office door of a professor of African American Studies, a university-wide convocation was called to discuss race relations on campus, the first of its kind in the institution's history. I was in my first month as the new dean of arts and sciences at the time and offered these words about racism and language.*]

Racism begins in language. It begins with words such as "we're coming to get you." Just as the Word became flesh, flesh also becomes words. This sacrament of language is reversible. Racism begins in language. *Understanding* racism, *repenting* of racism, *transforming* racism likewise begins in language. We are committed to this sacred principle because we are people of the word.

Some three weeks ago, *words* were written on a door, words that hurt people and threatened community. And what was our response? We needed more words. We should be grateful that the Black Student Union called for a rally at 10:00 a.m. on the steps of Presidents Hall. At that rally, a microphone was passed from speaker to speaker so that we, in community, could hear the word. However, those words — broken together in anger and angst, in perplexity and pacification — remained insufficient. We needed more words. We wanted to hear the president of our institution speak. And so the community reconvened three hours later, at one o'clock in the afternoon. Again, the microphone was passed from speaker to speaker, this time in the hands of the president. He spoke words. Students spoke words. After that rally, a private conference was held inside the administration building in order that more words could be spoken. And now, today, a public convocation is called to speak and hear the word. What began as language of hatred written on a door by an anonymous coward can become words of healing spoken in a hall by a community of the faithful. In gathering here, we are trying to work out our own salvation by redeeming the word.

There will always be naysayers among us who lack the faith, or who have lost the faith, to believe in this sacramental transformation of language. Words, they will say, are only words; talk is cheap. And we must be patient with their doubts. A history of racism in this country, at this institution, and in our own hearts has hardened the arteries of the body politic. To these nay-sayers, I extrapolate the wise words of Peter J. Gomes, revered minister of Memorial Church just up the coast at Harvard University:

> *The sentiment of some that [these words] are too little, too late, while ungracious, is surely understandable. This, though, is not about timetables, nor is it really about correcting a historical grievance; it is about how we [use] the [word], and about the creation of the moral imagination that allows us to do so. In that same moral imagination it is never too late to be right, or to be good.* *

We are people of the word at Seton Hall. We do not come here today to erase the language of hatred written on a door. We do not want to forget the words of bigotry shouted from dormitory windows. We cannot ignore lectures of intolerance uttered in the classroom. We are here to remember such words, and in re-membering them, by our shared faith, we can redeem them. We can transform them.

---

*Peter J. Gomes, *The Good Book: Reading the Bible with Mind and Heart* (New York: William Morrow, 1996), 101.

The incident that brings us together occurred toward the end of Lent, season of repentance. Now we approach the end of Easter, season of resurrection. Next week, we commemorate the beginning of Passover, season of God's most sacred promise.

 In re-membering words of bigotry we can transform them.

By transforming the languages of racism, sexism, classism, ageism, regionalism, nationalism, we can work out our own salvation together — in fear and trembling if need be, in anger and protest when necessary, in joy and dancing when possible.

We would like to be able to say "The word is risen," so that we can claim once again our communal "alleluia." But we may not be ready for that just yet. And it's okay to wait, to extend our season of Lent. Until such time as racism has been transformed — in our acts, in our attitudes, and in our language — we must hold fast to another word exchanged in daily sacrament with one another on this campus: "Peace be with you."

14

If Lent Is Spring Training
for the Soul, Who's On First?

The penitential season here in southern Illinois falls smack between the Fourth of July and Labor Day. That's when any afternoon below body temperature is called a St. Louis cold snap, and toweling off after a shower does as much good as spitting into a head-wind. If too-pooped-to-sin counted as spirituality, you could canonize the whole population from Effingham to Cairo during the dog days of late summer.

The real Lent, though, is another story. I suppose some pope, way back when, decided that mid-February to early April would be a dandy time for contemplating one's immortal soul. But I'll bet that pontiff never set foot south of Peoria, or he'd have thought twice before scheduling Lent when he did.

By St. Valentine's Day, we're turning over the soil down here — staking our raspberry shoots and tak-ing odds on whether the Cobden Appleknockers can go undefeated again this season. It can't be too long before some sober father in black suit and high collar shouts those glorious words of secular resurrection: "Play ball!"

For my money, this is what Lent's all about: spring training for the soul. It's six weeks of drilling the fundamentals — turning the double play, hitting the cutoff man, and timing the squeeze bunt — in preparation for throwing out that sacramental first ball of new hope. I'm sure "penance" and "pennants" only came to have different spellings because of some transcribing error.

Spring training for the soul is everything but fun. Whether you work out in St. Petersburg or Scottsdale, these six weeks are filled with spiritual trauma.

First thing every morning, the whole team masses together for doctrinal calisthenics. Then it's twenty-five wind sprints of self-denial, followed by world without end in the batting cage — praying to take a curve the opposite way, or to get full arm extension on the fastball. Afternoons are charitably spent in the field — running down pop-flying orphans and risking the tricky widow's bounce.

Visit any training camp, and you won't need a scorecard to tell the rookies from the veterans. Young hopefuls are the guys overdoing it, trying to impress the coach. They get to the ballpark an hour early and stay an hour late. They play on sore knees with welted bodies, actually preferring a little pain. The more they sweat, the happier they are. A rookie smiles all the time and says stuff like "just being here is what I've always wanted." To some old-timers, this kind of kid can be obnoxious and, truth be told, more than a little threatening in his devotion.

Visit any training camp, and you won't need a scorecard to tell the rookies from the veterans.

Seasoned pros can be spotted by their studied nonchalance, born of multiple trades and free agency. They chew a lot, spit a lot, and scratch a lot.

But, Rookies, beware. Late one night, after a few cold Buds, some grinning old pro may take you behind the grandstand and offer to sell you a couple of indulgences — maybe a strip of medium-grade sandpaper or a tiny vial of Vaseline. The only safe bet, given temptation like that, is total abstinence.

Your top class of ballplayer can be tricky to scout. The same holds with superstars as with saints: Being the real McCoys, they don't need to strut their stuff. They're loaded with natural talent and have developed it. They're dedicated from the word "go," always keeping both eyes on the ball, and never neglecting to run out a routine grounder. They're not threatened by rookies or worried about retirement. They possess drive and restraint in equal measure, have an aw-shucks humility, and are sly practical jokers in the clubhouse.

Three words go without saying in spring training, but they put the spin on every single pitch: Hall of Fame. Aspiring to make the hereafter is just as big a deal for ballplayers as it is for pilgrims.

Cooperstown is the heaven that dreams are made of. Sunday school children line up to gawk in awe at its sacred relics. Giving everything you've got in hopes of immortality is what spring training is all about. Just to make the roster pays the cost of any sacrifice.

Ditto for Lent.

I'm sure that some high-stakes holy-roller is going to protest my game as a sacrilege. But nothing could be further from the truth. If you can't see the miracle in a towering homer, or feel the new life of a hot smash caught right in the webbing, or hear the angelic choir in "Take Me Out to the Ball Game," there's fat chance you'll recognize resurrection in any other form.

The spiritual buoyancy of opening day is a foul tip off the bat of Easter's grace. It's the moment we dream of in the long off-season. It's the reason we deny ourselves through the hard spring training of Lent.

15

Language Fasting

Lent is a season of language fasting. For me, Ash Wednesday is marked more by the acoustic absence of "alleluia" than by the visual presence of an ash-smudged forehead. Throughout the liturgical year, we join to sing an alleluia in anticipation of the Gospel of Christ. Then suddenly, come Ash Wednesday, it's gone. We enter a period of enforced fasting. Attention must be paid.

Before the Lenten season, "alleluia" may become commonplace to us. We expect it in the Mass. We may even rise to our feet, singing the glorious word, while fumbling through a missal for the proper reading. Without thinking, we voice the word "alleluia," but we don't really utter (outer) it. It doesn't grow from deep inside us, joining the chorus of other worshipers to sing a harmony of communal praise. It hangs in the air, sterile, unconnected to the act of worship or to the guests at the feast.

If occasionally we trivialize "alleluia" during the weeks of Ordinary Time, this taking-for-granted comes home during Lent. For six weeks, the great word of praise is given a rest from its liturgical labors. It lies fallow, being nourished by reflection, in the hope of semantic renewal. In our language fasting, the "alleluia" dies. It is gone and buried, but not forgotten. As the weeks of Lent pass, we experience the genuine grief of an authentic loss. We ask forgiveness for our linguistic neglect. We hope for resurrection.

During Lent, in this enforced fast, a terrible pressure builds up in the vacuum surrounding Christ's Gospel. As Easter approaches, we experience the pain of deprivation; we feel the impulse to praise. Never again, we promise, will the "alleluia" be taken for granted.

Finally, during the Easter Vigil and on Easter morning, there it is again — resurrected, returned from the dead. Linguists would say that the word had become defamiliarized by its absence. It takes on a startling new appearance, a resurrection body. The historical Jesus, too, during the three days in the tomb, became defamiliarized, not immediately recognizable in his resurrection body.

At the Feast of Easter, "alleluia" is redeemed. The community of faithful breathes new life into the old word, and praise is resuscitated. At the announcement of the Gospel, we rise with Christ and sing, "Alleluia,

Alleluia. The Lord is risen. Alleluia!" The long season of Lent is over, and a new life has begun. Alleluia.

 As Easter approaches, we experience the pain of deprivation; we feel the impulse to praise.

Perhaps seasonal language fasting could redeem other words so important to our communal life of praise and worship — "Peace be with you," "Lord have mercy," "Hail Mary," "I love you." Authentic words, uttered from the depth of human emotion and hard experience, can be vital transmitters of grace. But they can lose their liveliness through inattention, neglect, or abuse. Language fasting, like the suppression of "alleluia" during Lent, reminds us of the living word and its need of nourishment. Language fasting, accompanied by semantic reflection, may redeem the vocabulary binding us to each other and to the Christ. Language fasting may even help to purify unholy discourse by illuminating the shallowness of everyday dis-grace: "Have a nice day."

16

How Do You Say
"Communion of Saints"?
Or, the Heresy of Verb Tenses

If you speak English, it makes it harder to believe in
the Communion of Saints. Let me explain. Speakers of
English cannot escape time — a prerequisite for grasp-
ing this theological doctrine — whereas the saints have
already done so. The Communion of Saints proclaims,
among other things, that, at the end of life, a Christian soldier gets reassigned regiments from "the Church
Militant" to either "the Church Suffering" or, optimally,
"the Church Triumphant." This does not deny the fact
of a person's biological death, just its finality. Thanks to
Christ's Resurrection, an individual's end is understood
to be a new beginning, in community with others. The
Communion of Saints asserts an ongoing, vital connec-
tion between the still-living and the living-again, that is
to say, the dead.

When referring to a deceased person in the natural world, grief counselors sometimes help survivors make the painful shift from present-tense references to past-tense reality: "Alas, she *is* no more; now she only *was*." Grammar helps us reach an emotional acceptance of a biological fact, and, apparently, the proper verb tense encourages us to get on with life. In a theological sense, however, a believer must transcend time to enter the realm of resurrection. God is eternally present, and so are the saints. Unfortunately, anyone whose thinking is conditioned by the rules of English grammar balks at this understanding.

Every English sentence demands a predicate, every predicate needs a verb, and every verb includes a tense — past, present, future, or one of those extra-credit, pluperfect variants. William Butler Yeats discovered this to his chagrin when trying to compose his visionary poems. In those works, perhaps one-fifth of his output, Yeats wanted to describe mystical experiences that occurred outside time. But he found the English language hampers communicating such ecstasy because it insists on the use of tense. Finally, Yeats addressed the problem by disguising verbs as gerunds, adding "-ing," then sneaking his action words into syntactic slots usually reserved for nouns. (Search among the parts of speech in his "Sailing to Byzantium," and you'll spot traces of time passing behind every port-hole, save the predicate's.) According to critic Louis Ceci, Yeats's visionary poems represent the best effort by an English-language writer to escape time, but he did it only by eschewing verbs.

As speakers of English, we refer to the living in the present tense and, naturally, we refer to our ancestors in the past tense. That is, the language insists on a divide that Christian theology does not recognize. "Dorothy Day...*was* the most significant, interesting, and influential person in the history of American Catholicism" (*Commonweal*). Or, closer to home, my grandmother *had* a great sense of humor. Both are dead and gone; yet each is alive and well within the Communion of Saints.

As I understand the doctrine, all saints ought to be referred to in the present tense. (By the way, speakers of Chinese and certain African click-tongues don't face this particular challenge to belief. Their verbs are free of mandatory time constraints.) In order to strengthen the faith of us the still-living, I recommend referring to all members of the Church Triumphant only and always in the present tense: Grandma *has* a splendid sense of humor. What's more, we needn't restrict references only to what we know of a saint's earthly life. We can extrapolate, through disciplined and faithful imagination, into our own present tenses.

One spiritual exercise I've adopted toward this end is to "invite a saint" as a partner in my reading. Recently, when devouring Stephen Greenblatt's *Will in the World,* I enriched the experience by carrying on a parallel dialogue with Wallace Bacon, an old friend and Shakespeare scholar who joined the Communion of Saints three years ago at age ninety. When enjoying David Lodge's *Author, Author,* I included my mentor Lilla Heston in the imagined re-creation of Henry James's life. Dr. Heston's tenure in the Communion of Saints began some twenty years ago, and I miss her still. While hearing Lodge and contemplating James, I communed with Heston in the full vivacity of the present tense.

So here's the plan: henceforth, let's refer to all the faithful deceased in the present tense, forever and ever. Amen. While not forgetting that they're biologically dead, recognize their eternal life, that is, their membership in the Communion of Saints, by a confident misuse of present-tense verbs. There's no reason why I should imagine Grandma lying lifeless under a marble slab when her vivacious voice can be giggling in my ear, adding joy to my days, calling me forward to my own hoped-for entrance into the Church Triumphant. After all, I would never refer to Jesus as "my late brother," because I know he *is* alive. And, because of his Resurrection, all the faithfully departed *are.* English grammar be damned!

LANGUAGE
and
WORK

17

The University Administrator as Novelist

I am a writer and a university administrator. I have authored nine books to date, with a tenth due to be published next spring. I was privileged to be dean of the College of Arts and Sciences at Seton Hall University, a college including twenty-one departments and sixteen research centers. Taken together, we spanned the physical sciences and mathematics, social and behavioral sciences, humanities, fine and performing arts, and interdisciplinary studies. Our college constituted a community of enormous intellectual diversity — multilingual, pluralistic, and global. I cherished no aspect of my identity more than full citizenship in this academic borderland.

In the two roles of writer and administrator, I see many similarities, although, at first glance, they may appear to share nothing in common. Specifically, I see a close kinship between the imperatives of trying to be a novelist and the responsibilities of trying to be a dean.

The conventional view of a university administrator is one who makes decisions regarding the allocation of resources and personnel, who gives directives when necessary to achieve organizational objectives, and who facilitates a shared academic vision among faculty colleagues.

Three prevailing metaphors represent these administrative functions. The first is administrator as "business manager." Within this paradigm, an administrator considers all resources as assets to be employed in accomplishing certain objectives. The student becomes a customer. Budgetary allocations are made with an eye to the proverbial bottom line. Administrator as business manager thinks in terms of profits and losses, revenue streams, and business plans. The positive values associated with a commercial model are efficiency, cost-effectiveness, consumer satisfaction, product quality, and workforce productivity. There are obvious negative values inherent as well.

A second prevailing metaphor is administrator as "military commander." Here the administrator shares information only on a "need-to-know" basis. Competitors become enemies. Resources become weapons to win battles; troop strength is calculated for executing strategic plans. Loyalty is demanded of all employees, just as loyalty is expected of a good soldier. Insubordination is not tolerated. Students become trainees; faculty become trainers; administrators are commanders. The values associated with a military model are control, hierarchy, chain of command, and winning. These values, like those associated with the business model, can be extrapolated to both positive and negative ethical consequences.

A third prevailing metaphor is administrator as "intellectual leader." Here the individual retains primary identification as a faculty member, applying his or her disciplinary expertise — scientific, literary, mathematical, or whatever — to the solution of organizational problems. This type of administrator looks at the "big picture," sees change as an opportunity for innovation, and monitors institutional vocabulary and values for their impact on learning, teaching, and research. Characteristics associated with this model include paradigmatic thinking, conceptual planning, and faculty consultation.

All three metaphors (actually, they're *similes* as I've presented them) — the administrator as business manager, as military commander, and as intellectual leader — along with the values embedded in their expressive vocabularies, are useful, and I do not stand in judgment of any of them. There are other fashionable alternatives such as administrator as politician, administrator as bean counter, administrator as coach, and so forth. However, I would like to suggest another, different but complementary metaphor, namely, the *administrator as storyteller.* I want to advocate certain values associated with this model as distinct from the more customary approaches to university administration.

Before exploring what I mean by this narrative model, I should first specify what I do *not* mean by it. All words are hand-me-down materials carrying the prints of previous users. Connotations stick to the sides of words like semantic adhesions and can prove toxic to future, alternative utterances. Among the connotations I would like to scrape off the sides of the word "storyteller," like the underwater barnacles from the sides of a ship, are "entertainer," "fabricator," and "Sophist." In other words, I do not mean that the university administrator should be an "entertainer," although we have all witnessed the administrator as clown, and I daresay I have played that role myself from time to time. Also, I do not mean that the university administrator should adopt the role of "fabricator," although, regrettably, we have all suffered under administrators who do not always speak the truth. And I do not mean to recommend the administrator as "Sophist" — one who is facile in analysis or slick in presentation, lacking substance or substantiation. The word "storyteller" may suggest any of these connotations, but I should like you to eliminate them from your mental dictionary for the sake of present analysis.

Among the connotations I would like to scrape off the sides of the word "storyteller," like the underwater barnacles from the sides of a ship, are "entertainer," "fabricator," and "Sophist."

I am using the word "storyteller" in its more common, more ancient, more sacred sense — the storyteller as keeper and interpreter of a meaningful tale, significant, not only to the teller, but, more importantly, to the community. In the case of a university, the administrator has the potential to be keeper and shaper of those sacred stories that enable a learning community to change, flourish, and replenish itself with nutrient power.

Consider the story behind the story, or the "story *of* the story," to borrow a phrase from the notebooks of the novelist Henry James. Any narrative has, minimally, six elements — character, action, place, time, theme, and audience.

When telling any of the multiple stories comprising university life, an administrator must first know the *characters*. Depending on the size of an institution, the number of characters contributing to its story may be very many indeed. Characters come and go, assume major and minor roles, stroll to center stage, and recede to the wings. In my college of arts and sciences there were approximately two hundred tenured or tenure-track faculty, a greater number of adjuncts and term faculty members, six thousand enrolled students, and many thousands of alumni. Among these groups arose the primary characters in the narratives that I was privileged to tell. A college's story may not embrace the scope of a Cecil B. DeMille epic, but the sheer size of the cast can be pretty impressive. To be a responsible narrator, one better know all the major characters by name, have a reliable index to the identities of minor characters, and, more important, have some idea of what each is thinking and doing. Faculty, students, and alumni place enormous trust in a dean to narrate their stories. Thank God, I was not the sole narrator of the college's story. But I was a primary narrator. There was no escaping that obligation. For me, there was no matching its privilege.

Second, the narrating dean must know the *action* of the college's ever-changing, dynamic story. What's going on in terms of teaching, research, professional service, campus citizenship, co-curricular activities, and behind-the-scene intrigues? And what are the meaningful patterns connecting sequences of action? Do these constitute plot?

Third, the administrator as narrator needs to be familiar with *place*. As one aspect of narrative setting, place is always the crossroads of meaning. Place, in the case of my college, included almost all the buildings on a fifty-eight-acre campus, affiliations with other universities and professional associations, far-flung alliances around the globe, and connectivity through cyberspace.

Fourth, a storyteller is responsive to and responsible for *time*, especially the tensiveness between past and future, tradition and spontaneity, history and innovation, business-as-usual and strategic planning. Perceptions of time are being altered dramatically by emerging technologies.

Theme, the fifth narrative element, derives from consensual vision and compelling point of view. The tried-and-true themes of university narratives include freedom of inquiry and expression, critical thinking, pluralistic dialogue, intellectual integrity, ethical and moral consequences, societal change, and cultural formation. The nuanced themes in a college's story change from day to day, month to month, and term to term. New characters, surprising plot twists, expanded places, and altered time all affect theme.

Finally, the storytelling dean addresses multiple *audiences*. Every time my phone rang, or the beeping computer announced a new e-mail, or the snail mail crawled into my office, or the next appointment arrived, or I sat down at a committee table, or I went to a college basketball game, or I enjoy another banquet, the person on the other end of the line, screen, page, desk, table, bench, or buffet was a potential audience for the college's story. These included predictable constituencies — faculty, students, alumni, parents, central administrators, potential funding agencies, major donors, corporate partners, and, frankly, society at large.

The six elements of narrative — character, action, place, time, theme, and audience — constitute the who, what, where, when, why, and to whom of storytelling. They also constitute the network of thoughts, relationships, and decisions of a dean's daily life.

It was an enormous privilege to tell the story of a college of arts and sciences. I loved doing it, every time, to every audience. It was also an enormous responsibility. In addition to the statistical *reporting* that a dean must do (i.e., budgetary accounting, enrollment targets and credit-hour generation, faculty productivity, and facilities management), I would argue that a dean *must* tell the story. In fact, to my way of thinking, telling the story is more important than reporting the data. It's more significant. It's more memorable. It's more empowering. It's more *educational.* (Recall that our English infinitive "to educate" derives from a Latin root meaning "to lead out." And leading out, surely, is a storyteller's task: "Follow me.")

When faced with a potential audience member, often appearing unexpectedly at my door or on my telephone, I asked myself, "What does this person need to know about the characters, activities, and themes of our college?" What will energize him or her? What will engage his or her interest and commitment? I tried to tell a piece of the story with appropriate detail, since the credibility of any story always depends on concrete details and not intellectual abstractions. Name names. Narrate activities. Specify themes.

Nobel laureate Toni Morrison, an academic neighbor down the road at Princeton, says, "We die. That may be the meaning of life. But we *do* language. That may be the measure of our lives." The most potent way available for human beings to *do* language is through stories. For a university administrator, as for any other narrator, storytelling is agency. It is an act with consequences.

The ultimate power of narration is as a way of seeing. Storytelling creates a literal world of metaphoric meaning. Hildegard of Bingen wrote in a letter to a monk toward the end of her life in the twelfth century: "What I do not see I do not know." Storytelling is a way of *seeing,* with the aim of engendering and sharing *knowledge.* For the college administrator, the role of narrator provides a wholistic opportunity to preserve and shape the sacred stories of a learning community.

18

The Executive's Scarlet Letter

Nathaniel Hawthorne embroidered a scarlet "A" into the fabric of Hester Prynne's character in his classic American novel, thus branding her an outcast in the Puritan society of seventeenth-century New England. A similar fate awaits today's executive in the corporate culture, only now the offending initial represents *audit* rather than adultery. The secular fear of audit may be just as frightening as the religious fear of adultery. Both labels are accusatory, calling for examinations of conscience and behavior. Both smack of dirty dealings.

Some might argue that "audit" is a neutral term, whereas "adultery" makes a moral judgment. But that distinction doesn't hold in everyday experience. When the corporate brass calls for an audit of Jones's books, word of this news spreads through the organizational grapevine with toxic results. Jones's co-workers are likely to respond just like Hester's neighbors — first pity, then piety, then persecution. The mere threat of an unscheduled audit, like the rumor of adultery, presumes guilt.

In olden times, shunning was the usual response to adultery; the same holds true for today's audit. Cultural members must avoid accusation. The Puritans followed rigid rules of decorum to preclude even a hint of sexual impropriety. Today's money managers are more likely to conspire together: "I won't call for an audit of your books if you don't call for one of mine." Or, more probably, "You dare not call for an audit of my department lest I call for one of yours."

 The secular fear of audit may be just as frightening as the religious fear of adultery.

This analogy between Hester Prynne's adultery and an executive's fiscal finagling has lost the sexism of Church Fathers keeping special guard against female offenders. Nowadays, in the spirit of equal opportunity, the SEC and the IRS know very well that men dicker with figures and women cook books in relatively equal measure.

My point is a simple one: whether the bottom line is virginity or liquidity, cultural values are demonstrated most clearly by a society's sanctions against their trespass. What we hold most sacred, we guard most jealously. The Puritans demanded that a damning "A" be worn on the dress of Hester Prynne. Today's equivalent is probably the "perp walk" of Kenneth Lay or Dennis Kozlowski played on the evening news or photographed for the front page of *USA Today*. I maintain that "Audit" represents the scarlet "A" of our corporate culture, and we're already parenting the Pearls of our future discontent.

19

Should Children's Literature Be Seen but Not Heard?

What I know about children's literature I've snagged by the seat of my pants. As a child, I didn't read fiction, sorry to say. In my parents' house, it wasn't a thing boys did. My father prided himself on not reading anything but *The Wall Street Journal* and the Chicago dailies. Mother, on the other hand, read treasure troves — a book a day, as I recall — but this didn't take with me. Living under her influence rendered me in the same position as a security guard I once met at the Guggenheim in New York City. After strolling though an exhibition of German Re-Figured Paintings, I asked, "Can you tell me what 're-figured' means?" She gave me the sweetest smile and, in a broad Brooklyn accent, pronounced, "I've only worked here for fifteen years. This stuff hasn't begun to rub off yet." I can't totally regret a childhood without novels. My days were full of narratives willy-nilly, gossip heard and overheard.

In consequence, children's literature became, for me, a pleasure deferred.

I didn't start reading novels of any ilk seriously until graduate school. But when I did, their impact on me was immediate and life-changing. Henry James and William Faulkner pummeled my imagination like a tag-team from Parnassus. I became aware of children's literature at about the same time. Ever since, I've pursued my readerly education in simultaneous private seminars — "The Contemporary Novel" and "Storying with Children." My notebooks blended the experiences of Charles Williams with Madeline L'Engle, Walker Percy with Jill Paton Walsh, Robert Coover with Robert Cormier, and Toni Morrison with Mildred Taylor. I took my history, in equal measures, from Terry Eagleton and John Rowe Townsend. I studied criticism with Wayne Booth as well as Aidan Chambers.

For half of my Ph.D. dissertation, I wrote a children's novel and, in the second part, included three critical essays analyzing the writer's changing relationship with an evolving text. These theoretical discussions drew upon the published self-critiques of some sixty American and British novelists, focusing particularly on Henry James, William Faulkner, Virginia Woolf, and Flannery O'Connor. Because such a project was unprecedented in the graduate school at Northwestern

University, it received close scrutiny through all its stages, from written prospectus through oral defense. It was in the latter — a two-hour discussion with a five-member faculty committee — that I first encountered an academic prejudice against children's literature. About an hour into the examination, a professor of literary criticism asked, "Do you really think Henry James would take an interest in a novel such as yours?"

I was prepared for his question and offered a modest rejoinder: "I do not pretend to compare my work with that of James, nor to suggest that the technical problems I face as an apprentice writer are identical to those of his mature talent."

"That's not my point at all," this professor corrected. "I'm sure James would be quite interested in another novelist's apprenticeship. I'm questioning whether he'd be interested in a *children's* book."

I must say this objection had never occurred to me. Fortunately, I wouldn't have to give an answer. The late Lilla Heston, my advisor and herself a respected James scholar, went on the offensive with an academic barrage like only she could launch. In her resonant baritone, she quoted James verbatim from several sources to demonstrate a general interest in all readers and a specific concern for children. I sat there in a candidate's dream, nodding my head in complete agreement with my advisor's critical attack.

When a year later I took my first job as an assistant professor, I ran into this same negative assumption, expressed now in different terms. I was assigned to teach a graduate course called "Children's Literature in Performance" — a class that my colleagues casually referred to as "Kiddie Lit." I took their double diminutive, belittling both the reader and the literature, as a personal insult and a political assault. I began an immediate campaign to change the language of our departmental discourse, explaining my rationale and monitoring their compliance.

I've thought lately about these two examples. What could possess an otherwise sensible professor of literary criticism to claim that Henry James wouldn't be interested in children's literature? Or, what might persuade a whole faculty, otherwise intelligent and sensitive souls, to demean their own curriculum by using a patronizing label? I'm prepared to posit this simple answer: children's literature, as a subject for serious inquiry, is politically suppressed. It suffers a benign neglect similar to that shown toward other minority literatures. Only in this case, the cultural silencing is more insidious.

In an age of deconstruction, when Marxism and feminism demonstrate how the cultural institutions of literature silence certain voices while privileging others, who in the academy stands up for children's stories and poems *as* literature? I can think of no other group of readers more politically suppressed or culturally exploited than the young. They are almost voiceless. They do not write, edit, or publish their own literature. They neither market it nor stock it. They do not review it, adopt it into library collections, or, for the most part, purchase it.

Young readers are not without their champions, I'm well aware. They'd be an endangered species for sure without the patronage of so many dedicated authors, editors, publishers, booksellers, librarians, and, especially, teachers. I acknowledge, too, the secondary function of children's literature within the reading curriculum of education programs. But that's a somewhat different matter.

Perhaps one reason why this genre and its history are so rarely taught in the English curriculum is because of its natural resistance to theoretical decoding. Aesthetic clarity (see Natalie Babbitt) and narrative simplicity (see most traditional fairy tales) defy criticism. Another reason might be the threat posed to university professors by children themselves. As Isaac Bashevis Singer reminds us, "[Children are] still the independent reader[s] who rely on nothing but [their] own taste. Names and authorities mean nothing to [them]."

While visiting the British Isles and enjoying an "Old Peculier Casserole" in a Yorkshire pub with Brian Alderson, I was lamenting this second-class citizenship of children's literature in the English curriculum. Alderson held that such neglect, all things considered, might not be a bad thing. "After all," he reasoned, "look what damage literary theorists have already done to so many classics."

I can think of no other group of readers more politically suppressed or culturally exploited than the young.

Fair enough. But I can't dismiss the issue quite so cynically. For better or for worse, leading members of English departments have become the Philosopher-Kings, deciding who warrants citizenship in the Ideal Republic of Literature. Plato, recall, rejected all imaginative writers on the basis that they were thrice-removed from truth and, when composing, they were not in their right minds. Nowadays, the literary establishment applies a somewhat different standard. Who's in and who's out can be a tricky judgment call. And those who make the decisions are becoming increasingly uneasy about their own accountability.

Under the aegis of artistic affirmative action and equal opportunity, the English curriculum is offering students new access to voices heretofore silenced or muted by cultural imperialism, male chauvinism, Anglo-racism, or academic elitism. When, one wonders, will this curricular enlightenment be extended to children's literature? When will the critical embrace be offered to young readers?

In little more than a decade, literary debate has moved from cultural confrontations over the canon to self-congratulations over the curriculum. Children's literature, however, is still patronized in the paternalistic house of fiction. If it behaves itself, performing courteously on demand, "kiddie lit" may be allowed to stay up late, nibble an hors d'oeuvre, and listen respectfully to adult talk. Should it try to assert its voice into the critical colloquy, Pater Theory and Alma Mater are sure to scold it for displaying bad manners: "Children's literature, don't you know, should be seen but *not* heard."

Fiddlesticks!

20

Discursive Messiness

The Pleasure of Being a Dean of Arts and Sciences

I was dean of a college of arts and sciences that included twenty-one departments, plus many programs and research centers. When I convened monthly meetings of chairs and directors, thirty-eight people were present, in addition to me. (This is hypothetical, of course. Perfect attendance at any regularly scheduled administrative meeting would be an absurd expectation.) These thirty-eight entities — departments, programs, and centers — clustered roughly around the sciences and mathematics, social and behavioral sciences, humanities, and fine and performing arts. We were big, this college of arts and sciences. We accounted for two-thirds of Seton Hall University by all measures save one. We had two-thirds of the faculty, two-thirds of the students, and two-thirds of the credit hours. Would that we had two-thirds of the budget. Nobody pushed us around.

That was kind of cool in itself, this collective swagger of ours, and it helped compensate in a small way for the fact that we were all underpaid.

I loved being a dean of arts and sciences. It was a real hoot. The college was peopled with passionate eccentrics, brainy neurotics, and only a few borderline-dangerous psychotics. We didn't have *factions* as, say, any self-respecting school of business is likely to have. We constituted an eclectic exhibit, not unlike the art collection of comedian and writer Steve Martin, recently on display in Las Vegas — all interesting pieces but lacking any common theme or discernible logic of acquisition. But the traits I've mentioned so far are not the best part of life in a college of arts and sciences. The best part, for me, is the discursive messiness created by any and all of our attempts at meaningful dialogue.

The sciences and mathematics, social and behavioral sciences, humanities, and fine and performing arts are rooted in disparate intellectual heritages, to say nothing of the constituent disciplines comprising these clusters. Each expresses itself in a distinct theoretical and critical vocabulary. Sometimes the words used by one group or another are actually different, comprising a unique language. Other times the same word may be used by different groups, but it carries quite separate meanings for various speakers. An example of the latter is the simple noun "paper." To a chemist or mathematician, a "paper" represents published scholarship, the end product of long research. To a professor of literature or a philosopher, a "paper" represents verbal presentation, the beginning of a research journey that may or may not lead to publication. Such an apparently simple distinction, which is in no way technical and merely draws upon the everyday parlance of co-cultures, can lead to a real donnybrook at a contentious meeting of the Tenure and Promotion Committee.

When debating academic policy, core curriculum, or criteria for merit pay in a college-wide assembly, in order for a physicist to make a nuanced point to a sculptor, in order for a professor of criminal justice to engage an Elizabethan scholar from the English Department, borders must be crossed, boundaries spanned. At such meetings, it was my duty from time-to-time to stand up and say, "Speak more slowly, speak more quietly. To get the most out of this dialogue, we're going to have to do a delicate act of translation."

My God, how I adored the result — this necessity for translation, border-crossing, boundary-spanning. Within the interdisciplinary multiculture of arts and sciences, all members in good standing must be at least bilingual, or, better yet, multilingual. To navigate a meaningful way through the discursive messiness occasioned by interdisciplinary citizenship, one *must* become fluent in plural tongues. If enough faculty members become adroit at transdisciplinary travel, speaking the languages of neighboring intellectual fields or, best of all, taking up permanent residency in the borderlands between disciplines, there may emerge a communitarian ethic coming darned close to utopia.

To get the most out of this dialogue, we're going to have to do a delicate act of translation.

It's the rare day that I envied the comparative hegemony of the school of nursing or, on my campus, the school of theology, where a much smaller number of faculty members all speak the same language. In trade-off for their discursive neatness and consequent efficiency, we lived it up in the carnivalized jazz of Bakhtin's *heteroglossia*. Our intellectual diversity, made manifest by discursive messiness, was emblematic of other dimensions of diversity within each individual, in all relationships, among groups, amid the campus culture as a whole, and between the university and its many neighboring communities.

The discursive messiness of interdisciplinary engagement, prototypically postmodern, is perpetually instructive. It's education at its best. *Ex ducare*: I am literally "led out" of myself and my provincial ways of thinking and seeing in order to take on the perspective, the language, of an Other. Life in the interdisciplinary multiculture of a college of arts and sciences provides a daily, living laboratory for examining and embodying cultural diversity. What I've tried to describe here, in a casual way, is not "interdisciplinary study" in the traditional sense of the term. Rather, I've tried to point to the studious *life* within a college of arts and sciences, especially as experienced in discourse. To me, the course of life made available in such a school, one's *curriculum vitae,* is worth paying full tuition.

LANGUAGE
and
WRITING

21

And Be a Writer—
On the Side

In an advanced creative writing course, one meets doctoral students testing their vocations, MFA playwrights working on full-length productions, and a few exceptional undergrads in love with the words and oblivious to the odds. Whenever discussion turns to career opportunities, several students may be counted on to announce, "I intend to teach college and to write *on the side.*" This declaration meets with nods of approval from fellow students and reflects, no doubt, the sensible cautions of parents or spouses. To be a writer *on the side* is a reasonable ambition. And to combine the teacher's profession with the writer's vocation would appear to integrate complementary careers. (Two roads diverged in a yellow wood, and I took them both.)

William Faulkner, remember, admonished would-be novelists to maintain their "amateur status" by pursuing another means of financial support. And John Gardner, in his posthumous volume *On Becoming a Novelist,* recommends college teaching as the most congenial complement to a writer's calling. To teach and to write side-by-side may address financial concerns (Faulkner) and may solve time problems (Gardner), but it presumes too easily the compatibility of teaching and writing.

To be a successful instructor in any university curriculum, one must give the illusion of knowing things. Students expect this, and colleagues believe it: a professor ought to display some certainty or, in disciplines where certainty is passé, some expertise in theory construction and refutation. From the illusion of knowing things derives authority. Authority, in turn, ensures respect and cuts down on the number of potential grade grievances. Knowing things is essential, in short, to a professor's personal and professional survival.

 To be a writer on the side *is a reasonable ambition. (Two roads diverged in a yellow wood, and I took them both.)*

By contrast, writing is impelled by the opposite assumption: one does *not* know a certain thing and needs or wants badly to learn it. Writing is not a pedagogy but an epistemology. From the writer's compulsion to learn something (to find out who done it or, more often, how a set of circumstances tests a specific character) derives his or her creativity.

A happy professor who writes *on the side* lives in an unhappy tension between needing to know things and needing to learn things. To develop fully either belief — that one knows things or that one doesn't — demands practice and discipline, keeping up one's guard. To switch perspectives at will is neither easy nor painless.

A second tension between teaching and writing punctures the casual air of "on the side." The professor must be, to some extent, master of materials, in charge of things within a controlled environment. It simply won't do to have a professor too often startled or hoodwinked by the unexpected in a classroom. Students rely on an instructor to manipulate variables, negotiate conflict, and keep the academic business in order.

Writers, by contrast, speak often of being mastered *by* materials, of studying submission. A muse inspires, a daemon possesses, and a character speaks. The writer, with disciplined availability, becomes a servant to the story's will, marked by its intractable intent.

The roles of master and servant require different work habits and distinct accountabilities. One who would be master by day (the teacher) and servant by night (the writer) celebrates a daily "feast of fools."

22

Writing-as-Performance
A Methodology of Assent

I believe that writing may be considered a performance event in at least three senses. First, and most commonly, it's possible to conceive of the writer, while in the act, as being some kind of performer. Whether the precise analogy should be actor, juggler, clown, or swallower-of-swords depends on whether one's name sounds more like Robertson Davies, Mario Vargas Llosa, Milan Kundera, or John Barth. If we conceive of a writer thus, the text which he or she produces becomes a record of performance. This is what Robert Frost thought — an old man at birth — and the idea predated even him. Romantics gave arrested performances of self-expression, modernists of self-construction, postmodernists of self-immolation, and, since classical antiquity, we've had the sacramental model of self-transformation. Much has already been said about the writer as performer by theorists from Richard Poirier to Jerzy Kutnik, and I believe a deal of good has yet to be uttered on this simile.

A second way one might conceive of writing as performance is, quite literally, *in the body* — a kind of Teamster's approach to fictive construction. Here the writer actually walks and talks, schlepping the load of composition in his (Ernest Hemingway's) or her (Grace Paley's) own body. (Both gendered parentheticals report to have storied on their feet.) The accounts in *Writers at Work* are replete with eyewitness affidavits from runners, hikers, swimmers, shouters, talkers, stammerers, and kibitzers — authors who literalize their performances kinesthetically. These are people who, at age six, could not perfect the first-grade ideal of reading silently. In due time, apparently, they gave up the horrific ghost, began moving their lips shamelessly, uttering their words audibly, and strutting their stuff to boot. (One of my happy contributions to pedagogy was to pay homage to this toddling tradition by creating a course titled "Writing-as-Performance" in which the only two rules were that students had to (1) write aloud, (2) while walking. That eccentric syllabus has migrated hugely, and surprisingly, to far-flung institutional and curricular settings.)

A third way to conceive writing as performance would cast the author in an ensemble collaboration with the reader. The prospect of both on stage together is so radically destabilizing of author-ity and so playfully affirming of literari-ty. This would appear true even after granting writers a privilege of scripting the rough scenario on which they may improvise.

The author says yes to characters, and, more important, says yes to the reader.

I'm not saying anything novel now, we may agree. Mainstream scholars such as Stanley Fish and Barbara Herrnstein Smith have authorized the reader in so democratic a fashion that today even Evelyn Wood could be endowed with a bill of rights from here to eternity. Still, when spotlighting the creative collaboration in stage-worthy metaphors, one stands a chance of catharting fearsome bugaboos, and no more's the pity.

Alongside the hypotheses of literary theory, we can document the same aesthetic phenomenon through the field work of performative ethnographers, conversation analysts, and those anthropologists who've rounded the Victor Turn.

No author understood his collaborative role better, or took his community citizenship more seriously, than the experimental fuddy-duddy, William Carlos Williams.

Listen to how he describes the narrative diagnosis of unschooled patients to the child psychiatrist Robert Coles, as the latter reported:

A kid is telling me what happened, and where it hurts, and what he does to make the pain better, or what he's tried to do. Some of those kids, they're playwrights, they're storytellers! They'll set the scene for you. They'll introduce other people, not just themselves; I mean, they'll mimic people, or try to use their kind of words. They'll say, "And then he said . . . and then she said . . . and then I said . . . " They'll work all that into their own list of complaints.

Do you see what I'm trying to say? I can't hear a kid talk like that and not be sprung — sprung right out of my own damn self-preoccupations. I'll pick up a good story or novel and the same thing happens: I'm in someone else's world, thank God. I'm listening to their words. My own words become responses to what they say — the novelist or one of my patients. We're on stage! I'm thinking of the moral seriousness [you can see] on the stage, a certain kind of exchange between people, where the words really are charged.*

---

*Robert Coles, *The Call of Stories: Teaching and the Moral Imagination* (Boston: Houghton Mifflin, 1989), 104–5.

Williams charts a mundane medical history as symptomatic of narrative interactions generally. And I'm suggesting, further, that even the silent reader — alone in one's bed or jostled by the subway traffic of rush hour — experiences the same creative collaboration, improvising *with* the writer on the stage of private imagination. Author Susan Cooper goes so far as to suggest that the personal unconscious may be visualized, literalized, in theatrical trappings:

> *The theater. Consider the image. A magical place, quiet and dark most of the time — sometimes for months on end, if its owner is unlucky — but a place which once in a while is brilliant with light and life and excitement. It lies there sleeping, closed up, its doors all locked — until suddenly one day the doors are open and you can go in, and find wonder and delight. That isn't a bad image of the unconscious mind.**

Or, to reframe theatrical imagery into cinematic, we might agree with screenwriter and novelist Michael Herr who, in an interview with Michael Kaplan for *Entertainment Weekly* (May 18, 1990), claimed that "readers really have the final cut. They always have. They

---

*Excerpted from Ms. Cooper's Anne Carroll Moore Lecture, delivered at the New York Public Library on December 29, 1988, and reprinted in *The Horn Book* (May–June 1990), p. 305.

shoot a kind of film in their head when they read a book."

Imagining this ensemble performance between writer and reader, the text, then, becomes their enabling script. Writing-as-performance is based in a methodology of assent. The author says yes to characters, and, more important, says yes to the reader. Such yea-saying is not mere modesty or some fuzzy notion of political ideology; it's an acknowledgment of one aesthetic reality. Narrative is communal.

By envisioning an author as co-creative with the reader, I'm not unaware of parting company. I believe that the history of literature is a multiple-choice quiz which may be read along two parallel lines: (1) a methodology of resistance, fathered by Plato and, ultimately, birthing deconstruction, or (2) a methodology of assent, described by Aristotle, enacted in dramatism, and nearly exhausted by phenomenology. The resisters see writing and reading as a process of *exchanging lenses,* looking at things first one way and then another. The assenters experience literature by *transplanting eyes,* literally seeing things through another's body. The aim of resistance is to clarify, to bring things into focus. The aim of assent is to internalize, to bring things into being. The second model, I'm telling you, is much harder. It demands, of both writer and reader, an actor's

discipline and a lover's self-sacrifice. It is, not coinci-
dentally, the way of the cross — putting on the mind of
Christ, in spades.

Writing-as-performance is theatrical, dramatic, and
collaborative. It's a methodology of assent, saying yes
to the conversational turn-taking of self and other.
It yields a creative folly and playful confidence by
which author and reader together may be enrolled in
a community of schlemiels on pilgrimage to glory.

23

On Gossip and Bull
Two Forms of Narrative Talk

Teaching a seminar on the novelist's creative process occasions the odd interview with local practitioners and fly-by celebrities. When Richard Russo of *Empire Falls,* nobody's fool, came to class, we asked him what childhood memories may have influenced his work. The answer came back without hesitation, "I was exposed in my father to an expert shooter of bull." Not two weeks earlier I was the subject of a similar interview and offered a similar response: "Gossip, particularly as overheard among women when I was a boy, engendered a love for story."

Gossip and bull are matched amenities. They're dirty words, both of them. Each provides information worth knowing and, maybe, using. Their performance requires artistry and rewards tour de force. They are audience-centered, every bit as hospitable as Macbeth or the White Queen and twice as much fun. To the novelist, they are musts. Despite this family resemblance, however, gossip and bull are hardly the same thing. A couple of novelists tracing their roots to one or the other are unlikely to write similar stories.

I don't mean by "gossip" the spreading of rumors, malicious or benign. That's called "libel," and one way to reckon the difference is whether the tale told is actionable in court. A gossip's facts are always straight. Another thing I don't mean by "gossip" is any story told with a wink. Irony and satire may be gossip's kissing cousins, but they're nowhere near becoming bedfellows. Gossip demands a straight-arrow logic calculated to educe belief. And I don't include as gossip anything preached, proclaimed, or publicized. This performance is strictly a chamber art.

Here are some things that "bull" *cannot* entail: verification, sincerity, sympathy, empathy, or whispering. Whereas a gossip never winks, a buller can't hold still. He's likely to twitch, snuffle, chew, or spit, showing off real expertise in facial combinations. Entry into the Hall of Fame requires the hat trick, three scores in a single sentence.

Gossip passes on information deemed interesting to the speaker and important to the listener. Bull is the other way around. Gossip leans toward understatement, always holding something back, modesty forbidding.

Bull hunkers toward overstatement, holding forth. Gossip demands belief, "Who'd have thought it?" Bull wants disbelief: "Who are you kidding?" When challenged, gossip cites its sources; bull steps outside. Both are verbal arts, but gossip is conversational, whereas bull is oratorical. Gossip exists in the narrative mode, bull in the dramatic. At least, that's what Aristotle told Alexander, who told Cleopatra, who told Buffie, who....

I'll bet that gossip and bull, way back when, were restricted to different settings — one in the house and another in the club. Long since, though, these cultural performances have hit the road. Now there's hardly a place or occasion that rules them out entirely. Certainly not the corporate boardroom, which breeds them both. The same holds for all committees, fraternities, sororities, and faculties. Political rhetoric is replete. Eulogies almost insist on one or the other. Even public prayer has proven amenable to each.

Some would maintain that gender predisposes, that women gossip and men bull. Daniel Webster (not *Danielle*) concurs. If CNBC did one of its dial-an-opinion plebiscites on the essential difference, this sex distinction would probably win hands-down. But a survey of personal experience comes up with too many exceptions. Linguistic crossdressing is so commonplace these days that male gossips and female bullers hardly

171

attract notice at all. The choice represents more of an aesthetic orientation than a genetic combination.

Since the verbal performances of gossip and bull are perfected by daily rehearsal, any novelist would be fool to walk away. These narrative materials, artfully delivered, are in the public domain and worth the price of admission. Far from infringing on copyright, the novelist provides a necessary service of transcription and transformation. Gossip and bull ask to be passed along. They measure their own success by repetition and embellishment, the rating points of an oral tradition.

Gossip leans toward understatement, always holding something back, modesty forbidding. Bull hunkers toward overstatement, holding forth.

I maintain that novelists can be categorized under the headings "gossip" and "buller" as insightfully as with the labels realist/romantic, modernist/postmodernist, traditionalist/experimentalist, or any other fancy-pants dichotomy. Mind you, I'm not talking about the characters created by a novelist. Presumably, any good storyteller could create both varieties. I'm talking about the work as a whole, the thing in itself — *das Ding an Gossip* or *das Ding an Bull*.

Let's start with the easy ones.

Ernest Hemingway? A buller, clean and simple. Not only were his novels bull, but so was his narrative theory. He claimed to be possessed of a "built-in, shock-resistant, [bull] detector" that guided critical judgment.

Eudora Welty? No problem. A gossip. She says as much herself in *One Writer's Beginnings*.

John Gardner? Buller.

Flannery O'Connor? Gossip.

See how neatly they all fall out?

Gertrude Stein. Did somebody say gossip? Wrong. Buller.

Henry James? Come now, my dear — a freebee.

The question can get tricky, however, with quick-change artists. John Barth is a buller disguised as a gossip. Norman Mailer, I'll wager, is a gossip disguised as a buller. Now, Alice Walker is another story altogether — a gossip who winks, then asks you to step outside.

I don't see why anthologies of American narrative don't trace the lineage of gossip and bull at least as far back as Hawthorne and Melville. Each is a cinch to classify. Students could grasp the idea quickly and would learn to comment critically on "The Comparative Techniques of Theodore Dreiser and My Uncle Teddy." Exams might include long lists of true-false, multiple choice, and questions for matching. Essay topics would be reserved for problem novelists such as William Faulkner and Willa Cather.

I suppose some academic crank will object that this schema of mine trivializes narrative distinctions. But if I had a mind to, I could tell you a couple of stories about that academic crank, and you might think twice before buying him wholesale again. Or I suppose you might quibble with the odd point or two in my disputation. To which I say, "Wanna step outside?"

24

Par in Golf and Art

The concept of par stands like a hazard between golf and most other sports. In baseball, basketball, or football, for instance, all that's required to win is to play a little better than the other guy. Both teams can stink on a given day, but one of them is still going to win. (Chicago Cub fans pledge allegiance to this theorem.) But, with golf, every player on the course can lose. You might argue that bowling is in that same league, that "300" stands out there like some sort of par. But the two notions are entirely different. One is an ideal spelling perfection; the other is a standard measuring competence. Plato was a bowler; Aristotle golfed.

Par is a way of thinking, really, an absolutist ideology. It's thoroughly patriarchal, delighting in distinctions. Par prefers justice over mercy any day of the week. It sets a standard for personal performance that demands recollection, hears confession, and assigns penance. Par resembles the Ten Commandments more than it does the Constitution: no interpretation required. Although it gives a favorable lie to Republicans, par matches up better with Hoyle than with Nixon.

The prevalence of par as an evaluative norm cuts across all types of endeavor. The batch of garlic grits I concocted last night didn't come up to par — too salty. I once owned an automobile called the "Cricket," which fell far short of vehicular par. Not a day passes without my hearing someone assessing something as "up to par," "par for the course," or "way below par." (Note: The language deserves a slight handicap here due to the fact that nongolfers share this metaphor equally with golfers. In everyday parlance, "below" is an indictment; in golf, it's a fantasy.)

Par is a normative paradigm that rank-orders items within a classification. It's a consensus judgment, for instance, that certain golf holes should be played in four strokes, others in three or five. Each number becomes a generic category under which particular holes on specific courses may be reasonably compared. Lacking such agreement, golfers could not compete. Trusting their collective wisdom will produce the leader board — a hierarchy of players distributed neatly along a scale from negative numbers to positive with par as the magic fulcrum.

This concept plays just fine for golf. I have some difficulty, however, when critics borrow par in order to tee off on works of art. They put a metaphoric spin on the ball that slices assessment well into the rough. Movie critics hail the latest release as above par or below par. Art collectors scramble for the longest drive and the best score. Book reviewers love to compare shots back in the clubhouse: "William Wharton is a birdie novelist, whereas Stephen King is only a bogey man."

You know that par has gone kaput when you see a player standing squarely on the sixth tee and taking dead aim at the ninth green.

When par moves from the links to the arts, it shoulders a bag of unwieldy clubs. In golf, the concept is fixed, knowable, and monitored by the USGA. With art, it's fluid, unspoken, and personalized by the interests of each critic. If a painting or a poem didn't measure up to par, I'd want the scorekeeper to announce what par was. If an orchestra's performance of Mozart's Second Symphony were deemed par for the course, I'd want to know where they were playing. Without some critical consensus, the concept of par cannot stay in the fair way.

In the past, it may have been possible to substitute genre for par — some agreed-upon classification with clear criteria for assessing artistic achievement. Hence, when a poet used to take aim at the Italian sonnet, his scorecard was well marked for distance, hazards, and out of bounds. Or when a pianist took a swing at ragtime, she knew where the ball was supposed to land. "Par for the course" meant something in a lexicon of artistic genres. But the whole notion is thrown out of whack on contemporary courses where the greens are over-seeded, the tees are provisional, and the competitors are encouraged to kick their balls.

For many playful artists, the bigger the hook, the better. They revel in the blurring of genres, even while critics keep scribbling all over their used and crumpled scorecards. You know that par has gone kaput when you see a player standing squarely on the sixth tee and taking dead aim at the ninth green. Today's writer of murder mysteries can shoot for philosophical profundity. The painter may delight in photographic clarity. Even the scratch essayist may choose to put so much English on the ball that it fades elegantly into the woods. Without clear genres, our normative jig is up. Par is a dated concept on an ahistorical course.

Barbara Herrnstein Smith speaks of the "Contingencies of Value" in contemporary literary criticism, entering match play on the side of artistic evaluation. She points out the hazard of generic classifications and the trap of normative paradigms. "Par for the course," when applied to art, has begun to strike out; it's a mixed-up figure stuck in the wrong game. We need new metaphors of assessment. Perhaps an image for the interim could be derived from Frisbee: what counts is the flick of the wrist, the spin of the disc, the pleasure of flight, the caprice of the wind, and the uncertainty of catch as catch can.

Acknowledgments

Several of the essays in this book appeared previously, sometimes in slightly different forms, in the following publications. The author expresses gratitude to the original editors for their encouragement, as well as to the current editors for permission to reprint.

"Kidnapped: From Baptist Playwright to 'Catlick'" in *Commonweal*.

"To Friends of the Library" (under the title "Freeport Library, His 'Holy of Holies'") in *The Freeport Journal Standard*.

"About Nintendo" in *Parents' Choice,* Parents' Choice Foundation.

"Death and Resurrection" in *The Humanist*.

"Vocation Education" in *America,* Republished with permission from *America* and americamagazine.org, July 1, 2002. Copyright America Press, Inc. 2002. All rights reserved.

"Moses, Hezekiah, and Yale's Gang of Four" in *The Reformed Journal,* © 1983 Wm. B. Eerdmans Publishing Co., Grand Rapids, Mich. Used by permission of the publisher.

"The Medium Is the Message" in *The Christian Century,* Copyright 1974 Christian Century. Reprinted by permission from the December 25, 1974, issue of *The Christian Century.* Subscriptions: $49/yr. from PO Box 378, Mt. Morris, IL 61054. 1-800-208-4097.

Acknowledgments

"The Word Became Flesh, Then Digital" in *National Catholic Reporter.*

"If Lent Is Spring Training for the Soul..." in *National Catholic Reporter* (www.NCRonline.org).

"Language Fasting" in *The Messenger.*

"How Do You Say 'Communion of Saints'?" (under the title "Saintly Grammar") in *Commonweal.*

Additionally, Rebecca Pepper Sinkler accepted both "On Gossip and Bull" and "Par in Golf and Art" for publication in *The New York Times Book Review* and offered instructive editorial advice, especially in regard to the tricky business of how to talk about "bull," a genre of narrative discourse, without inadvertently violating the list of taboo words not fit for print in *The New York Times.*

Of Related Interest

Robert Barron
HEAVEN IN STONE AND GLASS
Experiencing the Spirituality of the Great Cathedrals

Now in paperback!

This book combines both meditation and Christian art. Lovers of the sacred space created by Gothic cathedrals will revel in the spirit in which they were built. Christians interested in deepening their faith will find much nourishment as they ponder the depth of faith in God carved into the very stone of the cathedrals.

"Open this book and find yourself not only placed before great art, but also thrust into an encounter with the spirituality that created the art. Robert Barron has brought the sacred, mystical space of the Gothic cathedrals to our fingertips, and in so doing has also fed our hunger for God."   — *Spiritual Book News*

0-8245-1993-0, $16.95 paperback

crossroad

Of Related Interest

Steve Kissing
RUNNING FROM THE DEVIL
A Memoir of a Boy Possessed

A "hilarious" book (*Publisher's Weekly, Library Journal*), *Running from the Devil* is the poignant and bestselling memoir of one boy's struggle to make sense of his Catholic faith while he believed he was being possessed by the devil.

0-8245-2105-6, $22.95 hardcover

Please support your local bookstore,
or call 1-800-707-0670 for Customer Service.

For a free catalog, write us at

THE CROSSROAD PUBLISHING COMPANY
16 Penn Plaza, 481 Eighth Avenue
New York, NY 10001

Visit our website at
www.crossroadpublishing.com
All prices subject to change.

crossroad